Thy Will Be Done

God's Purpose in My Life

Alexander Isaacs

TEACH Services, Inc.
PUBLISHING
www.TEACHServices.com • (800) 367-1844

World rights reserved. This book or any portion thereof may not be copied or reproduced in any form or manner whatever, except as provided by law, without the written permission of the publisher, except by a reviewer who may quote brief passages in a review.

This book was written to provide truthful information in regard to the subject matter covered. The author assumes full responsibility for the accuracy of all facts and quotations as cited in this book. The opinions expressed in this book are the author's personal views and interpretation of the Bible, Spirit of Prophecy, and/or contemporary authors and do not necessarily reflect those of TEACH Services, Inc.

This book is sold with the understanding that the publisher is not engaged in giving spiritual, legal, medical, or other professional advice. If authoritative advice is needed, the reader should seek the counsel of a competent professional.

Copyright © 2013 TEACH Services, Inc.
ISBN-13: 978-1-57258-738-0 (Paperback)
ISBN-13: 978-1-57258-739-7 (ePub)
ISBN-13: 978-1-57258-740-3 (Kindle)
Library of Congress Control Number: 2012955183

Published by

www.TEACHServices.com • (800) 367-1844

Table of Contents

Preface v

Chapter 1   Tragedy Strikes 9

Chapter 2   The Nuclear Family Splits Up 14

Chapter 3   Seventh-day Adventism and Moving to Lyden 16

Chapter 4   Life in the Lyden Community 22

Chapter 5   Relocation to Long Creek 27

Chapter 6   In Touch With Adventism Again 31

Chapter 7   Conversion Experience 35

Chapter 8   In Service for the Lord 40

Chapter 9   Holy Spirit: Faithful Guide 44

Chapter 10   The Call to be a Pastor 49

Chapter 11   Sorting Out the Call 55

Chapter 12   Serving the Lord in the Classroom 60

Chapter 13   Where to Now? 68

Chapter 14   God's Providence 71

Chapter 15	CUC at Last 77
Chapter 16	A New Beginning 88
Chapter 17	Making Full Proof of My Ministry 106
Chapter 18	Providence at Work Again 109
Chapter 19	Life at Loma Linda 117
Chapter 20	Government Service 123
Chapter 21	Employment Decisions 126
Chapter 22	Serving the Lord Through Ministry 132
Chapter 23	Pastoral Responsibilities 137
Chapter 24	Stint with Caribbean Union College Extension Campus in Guyana 141
Chapter 25	Leadership Role at Davis Memorial Hospital 143
Chapter 26	New Responsibilities in the Caribbean Union 148
Chapter 27	God Is Not Finished With Me Yet 151

Preface

When I began writing my book, I had intended to compile a comprehensive family history. However, as my writing began to take shape, I came to the realization that that was too ambitious an undertaking. I, therefore, decided to narrow my book to focus on two major aspects of my life.

Firstly, for most of my life, particularly during my childhood and early adulthood, I kept hearing various versions of our early family life, particularly a major setback in the family that affected my family's well-being in significant ways from that point forward. But there were lots of misconceptions out there about what had actually happened.

Though only a child when the incident occurred, I could still remember quite vividly our family life in those early years. In a number of instances, what I kept hearing about the incident from some of my siblings, particularly the younger ones, which they no doubt had gleaned essentially from secondary sources, did not match with my recollections and what I knew from *personal* experience. With such misconceptions being peddled around, many people had hurt feelings, which resulted in the development of some degree of animosity among some family members. I felt a compulsion, therefore, that in the best interest of everyone concerned I should share what I knew about that early period of our family history in an effort to clear up those misconceptions by stating the facts as best as I could.

Secondly, my conversion to Christianity has been a most inspiring and fulfilling experience characterized essentially by numerous evidences of God's direct leading in my life and work. Taking a cue from Jesus' instruction to the man whom he had healed of the demons and told to, "Go … and tell … what wonderful things God has done for you" (Mark 5:19, TLB), I have decided to share my conversion experience. Being well aware of what God has done in my life over the years, my wife, siblings, and some close friends encouraged me to write about my experience.

Inasmuch as I was willing to write of my experience, I faced a major challenge. I did not know how to put together a book that would capture these two major aspects of my life. Where should I begin? I began exploring a number

Thy Will Be Done

of avenues through which such a feat could be accomplished. One day in 1998 while a graduate student at Loma Linda University, I was going through the mailbox at my apartment when I stumbled across a flyer from the Writers' Digest School (WDS) of Cincinnati, Ohio. I was tempted to discard the flyer as another piece of junk mail, but I felt impressed to at least skim over it before discarding it.

To my surprise it was indeed an actual promotion from WDS whereby they were offering a *Writing Your Life Story and Memoirs* workshop through correspondence. As I read through the brochure more closely, I noticed, to my delight, that a main feature of the workshop was that by the end of the course each student would have completed the first forty pages of his/her memoir or book. I could not believe my good fortune so, with no time to lose, and notwithstanding the demands of my study program at Loma Linda University, I enrolled in the course within a week.

I began the writing process with much enthusiasm. It was very exciting to see the work take shape. However, within a short space of time, I was forced to put the writing course on hold until a more convenient time and focus exclusively on my studies, which were becoming more demanding with each passing day.

After completing graduate school, I made several attempts to complete the WDS writing course and go on to complete my book. However, because of heavy work demands during the years immediately following my graduation, I just could not get around to doing so.

In 2005 while accompanying a group of students from Loma Linda University on a field school in the interior of Guyana, I was engaged in some deep reflections about my major life dreams and aspirations. At that point I made a commitment to get back to my writing course at the end of the field school. I even put together a timeline within which I hoped to complete the work. After the field trip I contacted WDS to see if I would be allowed to complete the writing workshop, taking into consideration the long lapse in time that had taken place. To my joy and delight, I was told that I could complete the course and even be re-assigned to the same instructor with whom I had begun the workshop. I was grateful for such an opportunity and soon picked up my writing again with even greater enthusiasm than which I had started earlier.

I stuck to my plan of completing the writing workshop, and with great determination and perseverance, I completed it well ahead of schedule. By the time I was through, true to their promise, I had indeed completed the first forty pages of my book. With the help of my WDS tutor's personal Writing Critique Service, I eventually completed the first draft of the manuscript. As

Preface

the manuscript was being edited for publication, I added a few more chapters.

Thy Will Be Done: God's Purpose in My Life captures some significant happenings in my early life and gives a firsthand account of the direct leading of God in my life's journey in my quest for meaning and direction. The major portion of the book highlights significant events in my life as these relate to God's guidance in the choice of my life work. It begins with an early family tragedy and then moves to some aspects of my early childhood, my conversion experience, my Christian life and work, my call to and ordination to the gospel ministry, and highlights of some aspects of my post-ordination years. The main thrust of my book is God's direction in my personal and professional life, particularly His guidance in helping me to sort out my call to the gospel ministry. The underlying message that I want to convey to my readers is that for the earnest seeker, God's will for that individual's life can be known and followed.

My primary purpose for writing this book is to inspire my readers to develop a nurturing faith and trust in God. I want my readers, especially those who are struggling to find out and follow God's will for their lives, to be inspired, motivated, and encouraged to exercise faith in God's leading and providence.

The theme of my book is: You can know God's will for your life.

The writing process itself called for a combination of good grammar skills and a flare for writing. I have discovered that good writing evolves and is best done during short periods or bursts of inspiration as opposed to a one shot event. My writing tended to flow best during those moments. What was of particular help to me in my writing was the possession of a good vocabulary, which helped me to find the most suitable words to express my thoughts and ideas in a manner that would "get my writing across" to my readers.

The sources of information used in the compilation of my book were excerpts from my personal diary, personal reflections, and interviews with family members. I was amazed at the degree of detail that I had actually captured in my diary and how that information enhanced my writing.

I would like to thank the following persons who helped me during the research, writing, and editing of my book. Firstly, a special thanks to my wife, Andrea, for her understanding and encouragement throughout the writing project. Secondly, to my father and siblings who regularly nudged me to complete the book and helped to clarify specific details on the content of the first two chapters. Third, a very special thanks to Arline Chase, my Writer's Digest School workshop instructor, who piloted me through the entire writing process that resulted in the completion of the first draft. She was also instrumental in helping me fine tune the title of my book. Arline is an excellent writing

Thy Will Be Done

instructor. An extra special thanks to Kalie Kelch, editor at TEACH Services Inc., for her expert and comprehensive editorial work on the manuscript in preparing it for publishing. Heartfelt thanks to professor Roy I. McGarrell for proofreading the book. Without their support, this project would not have been realized. Above all, thanks to God for helping me to complete this task.

Alexander Isaacs
May 28, 2012

Chapter 1

Tragedy Strikes

I had no idea when I awoke that morning that my life would change forever. Until then I had taken everything in my life for granted. Dad worked, and Mum stayed at home and took care of us. But on the day that everything changed, I was staying with my grandmother because my mother was sick. No one was too concerned about her illness. Staying with my grandmother was a temporary arrangement, and I expected everything to be back to "normal" in a few days.

Our normal life was a happy one. We played together and ate the delicious meals that Mum prepared daily. Early in the mornings we would visit the farm at the back of the house to gather mangoes that had fallen during the night. Dad left home for work early each day, so Mum got us ready for school. She prepared our meals, packed our lunches, and ensured that our books were safely placed in our bags.

In the afternoons after school, my siblings and I came home as a group. Each one of us was eager to fill Mum in on the happenings at school during the day. Somehow Mum listened to each story we had to tell. She was the first to know of anything that was bothering us. Her presence in the home brought a sense of security to everyone. With our mum around, life seemed a perpetual period of bliss.

Some evenings after Dad came home from work we would play "hide and seek" or the "boggie man" with him. When he played the "boggie man," he would cover himself with a sheet, get on to his knees, and chase us around the house. This brought much excitement and laughter to our home. Sometimes pandemonium would break out as each one of us would try to evade Dad's advances as he neared the area where we were hiding. Occasionally he would grab at us and catch one of us in his grasp. We would scream while in his grasp, but once he released his grasp, we would scamper away.

On moonlight nights our family would sometimes gather on the front steps, and Dad and Mum would tell us stories.

My family was comprised of five girls, two boys, Mum, and Dad. My eldest sister was short and chubby, and from time to time she would let the rest of us

Thy Will Be Done

know that she was the eldest one in the family. Whenever her authority appeared to be threatened, she would say, in a hurried expression, "You must respect *me*. After all, *I am* the big one." And that was enough to bring us back in line in most instances. She was a favorite of Grandmother Arhoda, my Mum's mother.

My second oldest sibling was two years younger than my eldest sister. She, too, was short and stocky in build. At school she stood up for us as her younger siblings if other children tried to take advantage of us.

I was the third child in the family, and I was the tallest. My parents said that I got more of the dominant genes from my mother's side of the family than from my dad's side. Dad said that he was so excited when I was born. As his first male child, soon after I was born he took me to his father and asked him to give me my full name. So my grandfather named me Alexander Agustus Isaacs, after himself.

The next one in line was my brother, one year younger than I. Growing up, he did not betray you easily if it meant being spared from disciplinary action from Mum or Dad. He was also stocky in build and did not mix matters when it came to meal time.

The next three babies to join our family were girls. Our fifth sibling, who has since passed away, was two years younger than my brother. Of all the other girls in the family, she resembled Mum the most, but she grew up to be a little taller than Mum and my other sisters. She was very reserved and did not say very much unless that became absolutely necessary.

The sixth sibling bore some semblance to her other sisters, but she had some prominent features of Grandmother Johannah, my father's mother.

The baby of the family was about three months old at the time that our lives changed forever. As the youngest sibling, we all fussed over her and were ready to do whatever was necessary to ensure her comfort and safety.

The Christmas feeling was beginning to fill the air. Carols were played over the airwaves. During this period in Guyana's history, Christmas carols hit the airwaves around the second week in November each year.

Christmas observance in my family was always a grand and much anticipated occasion, and my family was planning to make that year's celebration a truly memorable and enjoyable one. Excitement and eagerness filled the hearts of everyone within the home circle. There was much chatter about what presents Dad would buy for each child and how he would surprise us with those presents. We talked about how our home would be specially decorated, how many pounds of cake mother would bake, and on and on.

Mum, a seamstress for many years, had planned to make something special for each of us as Christmas gifts. It seemed that the closure of school was so far off, even though only a couple of weeks remained before the doors of the school would be closed for the Christmas holidays. We could hardly wait for Christmas Day to arrive.

But our dreams for a festive Christmas celebration that year were dashed with the rude and untimely intrusion of a death in our family. It came suddenly! Death, with its icy hands, fastened its tenacious grip on my mother and took her life.

I still vividly remember Dad paying us a visit at Grandmother Arhoda's house that fateful evening. As he walked into the yard, the look on his face immediately told us that something was wrong. His eyes were red; he appeared absentminded and was holding a crumpled up handkerchief with which he dried an occasional tear that slid down his cheek. As he made his way up the steps, he carried the bag that my mother had taken to the hospital. Upon seeing him, Grandmother clutched her heart and blurted out, before Dad could utter his first words, "How is Elfreda? Is she all right?" With sadness in his voice, Dad broke the news of Mum's death.

Dad recounted the events of the day. Earlier that day he had paid her a visit at the hospital. At the end of their visit, they were both in high spirits since her condition seemed to have improved markedly. He held her in his arms and kissed her goodbye. He then left the hospital to get her some more clothes before the afternoon visit because the clothes she had taken with her to hospital had to be laundered. But, by some strange turn of circumstances, when he returned to the hospital with the clothing four hours later, he discovered that she was not in the room where he had left her after the mid-day visit. When he inquired of her whereabouts, the nurses on duty took him aside and told him to sit down. Looking at them out of the corner of his eyes, he suspected that something was wrong. The nurses spoke in subdued tones and cast occasional glances at him. From the somber appearance on their faces, Dad got the feeling that Mum had probably gotten worse.

After a while, the senior nurse walked slowly across the room, placed her hands on his right shoulder, and said, "Mr. Isaacs, I do not know how to tell you this. Your wife died within an hour of your departure from the hospital after the noon visit."

What happened immediately after the nurse broke the news to him is lost from my dad's memory. All he remembers was waking up on a bed with several nurses around him fanning him. He had fainted upon receiving the news of my mother's death. As he recounted this incident, he sobbed between words.

My mother's death came as a shock to everyone. Grandmother Arhoda wailed aloud. My two older siblings cried without restraint. Soon my grandmother's house was filled with relatives, friends, and neighbors who heard the wailing and came to inquire about the cause. On learning of my mother's demise, they joined in the lamentation. I stood by passively observing all the commotion that was taking place and not knowing what to make of this sudden outburst.

On the day of the funeral, I was dressed in a brand new white shirt and black short pants that reached just below the knee. Mum's body was taken to Grandma Ahroda's residence and placed on stools in the front yard. My grandmother could not contain herself. As the coffin was being hoisted into the yard, she stood up and began crying in loud tones. She fainted several times and had to be revived again and again. While my adult cousins and friends mourned the loss, I merely stood on tiptoes and peered into the coffin; then I ran off to play with some friends who were at the funeral. The full extent of my mother's death did not strike me then.

After the funeral we returned to our grandmother's home where we stayed for a brief while. Dad's intention was to keep the family together as a unit. Thus, after a few days we were all back together at our home.

With Mum not around, things in and around the home were not the same. The cohesion within the family began to break up. School life was interrupted. My two older siblings took care of our baby sister as best they could. However, they could not provide the specialized care she needed. Dad prepared the meals for the family. Occasionally, a family member would pay a visit to our home to see how we were managing. But, for the most part, we were left to fend for ourselves.

Interrelationships within our extended family became strained when Mum died. Grandmother Arhoda and other members of my mother's side of the family blamed Dad for her death. The family felt that he had been negligent in protecting her from the elements, especially after giving birth to my baby sister. (It is believed in some circles here in Guyana that if a woman is not properly taken care of after delivery of a child and is not protected from direct exposure to drafts of cold air she could contract pneumonia, which is commonly called "lining cold" in the local dialect.) According to discussions with some family members, they believed that this was the reason for Mum's death. Dad denied the accusation and insisted that the real problem was that Mum's relatives had never favored him. The stalemate between Dad and our extended family did not in anyway benefit us. Dad was, therefore, left to bear the brunt of the responsibility in caring for the family.

"When you don't have luck, it is a bad thing," he would say whenever we would talk about what had happened.

Tragedy Strikes

As the weeks went by, Dad found it difficult to balance work and care for our family. It soon became apparent that, in our best interest, some major decisions needed to be made and made quickly. Sadly, these decisions had far-reaching consequences for our family.

Chapter 2

The Nuclear Family Splits Up

After a while—I cannot remember how long after Mum's death—Grandmother Arhoda called together some key members of our extended family to discuss our future well-being. Apparently no one gave thought to coming up with a solution that would keep us together as one unit or no one was prepared to take on a responsibility of such magnitude. It was eventually decided to have different persons adopt my siblings. Dad opposed this move because he wanted to keep the family together at all costs. However, with five girls ranging in age from 3 months to 10 years and two boys, 6 and 7 years old, to care for without support from the extended family, he eventually gave in to the demands of his in-laws.

The first to go was my baby sister. One of my cousins, Alfred Bryan, a lawyer's clerk residing in the capital city of Georgetown, agreed to adopt her. Even though dad put up heavy resistance to this move, he eventually gave in under pressure. According to Dad, he was threatened with having to raise all the children on his own if he did not agree to give up my baby sister for adoption.

Cousin Nina, who resided at Bartica, a rural mining community more than fifty miles away, adopted my fourth sibling.

Every time a sibling departed the ranks of the nuclear family, we all sobbed. It was as though a part of each member was being wrenched off and that there was no foreseeable way for the family unit to regroup into one whole again. Dad did his best to console us at those times, even though he felt the agony of separation much more than we could ever imagine.

My father spoke with his mother, Grandmother Johannah, and she agreed to adopt my sixth sibling. According to Dad, his side of the family was also not inclined to adopt or assist with the raising of any more of my siblings.

The rest of us—the eldest, 11, the second eldest, 9, my brother, 6, and myself—remained with Dad. We split our time between Dad, Grandmother Ahroda, and some family friends for varying periods of time. I remember my Dad having to pay a neighbor for the menial task of combing my two older sisters' hair on a daily basis so that they could go to school properly groomed.

Grandmother Arhoda eventually took over the raising of my eldest sibling, and not long thereafter, my second sibling was taken in by one of my dad's relatives who lived at Wales, a village approximately seven miles away.

Again, since Dad had to be at work during the day, my brother and I stayed with different relatives and friends for varying periods. Grandmother Johannah took us in for a little over a year during which time I was able to continue regular schooling. Unfortunately, for some unknown reason, there was a falling out between my father and Grandmother Johannah. Consequently, my brother and I were not allowed to stay at her home any longer.

In the meantime, my eldest sibling had moved to Poudroyen to attend secondary school and was staying with one of my father's relatives, Cecilia Haymer, who lived in that village. Faced with the challenge of keeping my brother and me with him, Dad arranged with Cousin Cecelia to take us in as well.

Thus, within two years of Mum's death, the family unit had disintegrated. Our identity as a nuclear family was nigh lost. We were all on our own, having to cope with growing up outside the safety and comfort of the once-happy nuclear family. Sadly, we had no regular contact with each other. Further, some of my siblings were deliberately isolated from the rest of us, and in many instances, from Dad. The most that could be done was hope for the best.

As I prepared to move to Poudroyen, I felt a great degree of uncertainty about what lay ahead.

Chapter 3

Seventh-day Adventism and Moving to Lyden

Life at Poudroyen was meaningful. Cousin Cecelia welcomed us with open arms and did whatever she could to make us comfortable. I began attending primary school once more on a regular basis.

Cousin Cecelia lived on the front lot while her only son, Cyril, lived with his family in a house on the back portion of the property. Since some of Cyril's children were of the same age as I was, I had many opportunities to play and develop special familial relationships.

Cousin Cecelia was a Roman Catholic. On select Sunday mornings my two siblings and some of my cousins would accompany her to church. I enjoyed dipping my fingers into the receptacle with the "holy water" just as you entered the church and bowing slightly as I made the sign of the cross, just as the other worshippers were doing before taking their seats in the pews at the Marlgtout Catholic Church, which was about five minutes' walk from Cousin Cecelia's house.

My cousins and I took pleasure in playing games such as cricket and hop scotch. On occasions we would get away from home to swim in the Bella Dam trench. This small waterway drained some arable agricultural land. During the summer I would ride a donkey to go down to a portion of those farmlands that had many mango trees. We would pick mostly half-ripe mangoes and fill several sacks. These were then placed on the donkeys and taken out of the mango estate. Once we got out to the front, a splash in the waters of the Bella was inevitable. I often climbed up on the Koker, which regulated the flow of the water to the farmlands, and plunged into the murky waters of the Bella.

Cousin Cecelia taught us lessons of thrift and respect for the elderly. When she found some spare time, she would sit us down and tell us about our ancestors, particularly from my father's lineage. I was thus able to learn of my ancestors by listening to the stories that Cousin Cecelia told us.

One yearly feature I looked forward to while living at Cousin Cecelia's was the annual fair staged on the grounds of the Roman Catholic Church. There was a wide variety of games for each age group. The prizes up for grabs made

Seventh-day Adventism and Moving to Lyden

us want to play continuously, for there was always the possibility that you might somehow become lucky. Whenever I won at one or more of the events, I jumped for joy. In addition, there was also a wide variety of mouth-watering foods and drinks on sale.

On Saturday mornings I went to the Village Market with Cousin Cecelia. She had been allocated a portion of space at the Village Market. I can still remember quite vividly scenes from the market. We would all get up early in the morning and help Cousin Cecelia fetch small bundles of vegetables and ground provisions out of the house to take to the market on her donkey-drawn cart. Getting to the market early was important if you hoped to have all your produce sold by mid-afternoon. The villagers arrived early to buy the best of the produce available.

After market, we would return home at around half past two in the afternoon and spend the rest of the day doing menial chores or running off to play.

One Saturday afternoon after we came home from market and the extended family was having a snack, there was a knock on the door. My eldest sister opened the door, exchanged a few words with the visitor, and then called Cousin Cecelia to speak with the individual. The middle-aged woman was Sister Bruce, a well-known Seventh-day Adventist from the same village. After a short exchange between my cousin and Sister Bruce, Cousin Cecelia informed us that Sister Bruce had invited us to attend Branch Sabbath School at Phoenix Park that same afternoon.

The Vreed-en-Hoop Seventh-day Adventist Church conducted the Branch Sabbath School as one of its outreach activities to the community. Since we had some free time on our hands, a few of us took an early bath, dressed in casual clothing, collected an offering from Cousin Cecelia, and went to Branch Sabbath School.

When I arrived at Branch Sabbath School, I saw many children there. They were singing choruses and clapping their hands cheerfully. I took a seat on one of the wooden benches under the two-story building where Branch Sabbath School was being kept and joined in the singing. I enjoyed the song service very much. After the singing of choruses, we were taught a Bible memory verse before listening to a Bible story. The teacher used a large four-foot by two-foot Picture Roll to help make the story come alive. On each page of the Picture Roll was a large picture that illustrated the main thrust of the story.

We all listened attentively. As the story unfolded, one child, unable to contain herself any longer, exclaimed "Miss, I know this story! My mummy read it to me and my brother."

Another blurted out, "Miss, what will happen to the boy? I can't watch

Thy Will Be Done

this!" Then the little girl placed her hands over her face and peeked through the spaces between her fingers, with eyes half closed, to see what the next picture was all about. When nothing serious happened to the character in question, the child breathed a sigh of relief.

The teacher then called on two of the children to pick up an offering. She then told us what to expect at Branch Sabbath School the following week. After a brief closing prayer, each child was given a light snack of juice and cookies. As the children filed out of Branch Sabbath School, they looked back and waved to the teacher, repeating again and again, "Bye Miss, Bye Miss," to which the teacher replied, "Bye! Bye! See you next week! Remember to bring a friend with you next week."

I returned to Branch Sabbath School the following Saturday afternoon, and before long this became a much-looked-forward-to-activity every Saturday afternoon. I took care to leave the market early enough to get to Branch Sabbath School on time as I did not want to miss out on any portion of the program. The caring ways of Sister Bruce, the Branch Sabbath School director, and her helpers impressed me greatly.

After attending the meetings for sometime, I developed an interest in what was taking place. Before long I was invited to attend the Saturday morning church services. I got permission from Cousin Cecelia to attend the morning services, and, for the first few months, I did so sporadically.

Thus began my acquaintance with the Seventh-day Adventist Church. My involvement with this body of Christian believers would take on broader and deeper dimensions in the years ahead.

I cannot remember the actual length of time I spent at Poudroyen, but it must have been a little more than a year and a half. I have fond memories of my stay at Cousin Cecelia's.

Unfortunately, just as I was beginning to settle into my new school and settle down at my cousin's house, she called my brother and me together one evening after supper. She wore a serious expression on her face, and then she said, "I have to send you back to live with your father." I could not believe what I was hearing. She continued, "It has been some time since I last heard from him. He hasn't brought any money recently, and what little I have is almost gone. Besides, the best place for boys to be is with their father. I recently spoke to one of your aunts, and she knows where your father is living. I will send you to her so that she can take you to the Georgetown Ferry Stelling and put you on a boat to go to your father."

I lingered around the house, trying to find something to do other than packing my things for this sudden move. *Cousin Cecelia might change her mind after all and let us stay*, I surmised.

"Come on boys, you do not have all evening to pack. And, besides, it is getting late. You must leave for your aunt's residence before nightfall."

I reluctantly packed my bag and said goodbye to Cousin Cecelia and the life I was beginning to enjoy there. My brother and I walked to our aunt's house about five miles away.

We arrived at our destination at around dusk that Sunday evening. Our aunt gave us a light supper and showed us to the room where we would be spending the night. As I drifted off to sleep, I felt a deep sense of foreboding about what the future held.

Very early the following morning, our aunt took us to the ferry by bus. I clutched my large paper bag, which contained a few pieces of clothing. As we passed by the village of Poudroyen, which was on the route to the ferry, I glanced down the street where Cousin Cecelia lived. So many fond memories of life at Poudroyen flooded my mind. My eyes filled with tears. Before long I was wiping the tears from my eyes with the back of my hand, trying my best not to let my aunt see me crying.

The bus on which we were traveling finally came to a stop at the Vreed-en-Hoop Ferry Stelling. The other passengers began to disembark, but I did not stir. I was oblivious of what was happening around me. My mind was at Cousin Cecelia's. "Come on, get up from your seat. We are at the ferry, boys," my aunt remarked. At her words, I dragged myself from my seat and disembarked the bus. She bought tickets for the three of us, and we crossed over on the ferry to Georgetown, which was on the other side of the Demerara River. The journey took us no more than twenty minutes.

Aunt Ina took us to the waterfront where the boats that plied the Demerara River were moored. My father lived up river with my stepmother in a village called Lyden. My aunt was in the process of negotiating our trip to Lyden on a particular boat when someone remarked, "Look Samo." "Samo" was my father's "call" name. Turning my head, I saw Dad approaching. As if by providence, he was getting ready to make the return trip up river. A mere glance at us with our large paper bags tucked under our arms with our meager belongings and the look of desperation on Aunt Ina's face told the story.

I was overjoyed to see Dad. Aunt Ina told him that Cousin Cecelia could not keep us any longer and that she had decided to send us to stay with him.

This sudden intrusion into Dad's world must have sent shivers up his spine. How would my stepmother react to Dad taking two of his children to live with them without first discussing it with her? Would she object to our living with them?

Thy Will Be Done

Dad decided to take us with him to Lyden. He took our bags and sat us down in the ferry boat. He then left to complete some outstanding business. When Dad returned to the boat, he brought us snacks. This was a most welcomed gesture.

I sat quietly on one of the wooden benches of the *Champa Devy, the ferry boat that was about to sail up river*. Some passengers sat on the seats while others spread sheets or blankets on the floor of the ferry in preparation for sleeping during the lengthy trip. Food stuffs and other cargo were stacked at different places on the boat.

Finally, the captain sounded a horn signaling the departure of the ferry boat. As the ferry boat moved away from the waterfront, family members on land waved goodbye to their loved ones on the boat. Some adventuresome passengers deliberately chose that particular moment to jump from the Stelling onto the boat to the delight and applause of those already on board.

During the trip, people ate, slept in a scattered manner on the floor, and conversed on a variety of subjects. I looked at the boat as it moved through the waters, the Lister inboard engine giving a rhythmical sound as the boat moved along. As we passed certain landmarks along the way, Dad filled us in.

Even though I was glad to be with Dad, I felt uneasy. My mind was preoccupied with the kind of reception that we would receive from my stepmother. Would she welcome us with open arms or would she reject us? Was she tall or short; beautiful like my mother or not? What would life be like in a new village with my new stepmother?

At different villages along the trip upriver, the passengers would signal to the captain when they were nearing their destination. The captain in turn would signal the engineer by pulling on a cord that held a bell at one end. Each sound of the bell and the intensity of that sound evoked a different response from the engineer who regulated the speed of the boat before bringing it almost to a stop.

At each stop along the route, I wondered if we had arrived at our final destination. I expressed some anxiety as to whether or not I would be able to climb down from the launch into the smaller boats that came by to pick up passengers who were disembarking. Looking at those small boats bobbing up and down on the water, occasionally taking in some water, did not help in the least.

By the time we arrived at Lyden, Dad's new home, it was already dark. The launch slowed to an almost dead stop in front of the house where Dad lived. As the boat drifted upriver with the tide, someone came out to meet us with a small boat. Dad got into the small boat first and then took us onboard one at a time. Being in Dad's arms felt safe. The boat then took us ashore.

Seventh-day Adventism and Moving to Lyden

My stepmother was not at home when we arrived. Dad gave us supper and then showed us to a room at the rear of the house. I was not merely tired from the trip but was anxious about what the new day would bring forth. I lay there in the dark thinking about my new stepmother and the look on Dad's face when he first saw us. He hadn't seemed all that happy about our return under the prevailing circumstances. I wondered what his new partner's reaction was going to be. Before long I pulled the sheet over my body, turned over in my bed, and drifted off to sleep.

Chapter 4

Life in the Lyden Community

The next morning after the trip up the Demerara River I was awakened by the sound of a rooster crowing in the backyard. I turned over in my bed, rubbed my eyes, and lay on my back. The consciousness that I was in a new environment suddenly struck me with great force. Since the boat had dropped us off at Dad's during the night, I had not had an opportunity to scout out our new surroundings.

"Boys, come out and meet your stepmother, and let's have breakfast," Dad said with one breath. I came out of the room in my navy blue pajamas, followed closely by my brother, and we greeted my dad and stepmother.

"Good morning, Daddy and Mum, er, Aunty, er…." There was silence. A smile crossed my stepmother's face. I did not know what name to call her by. "You can call her Cousin Rachael," Dad said, breaking the silence. My stepmother returned our greetings, "Good morning, boys." After a brief exchange, we had breakfast together.

Cousin Rachael's mom, fondly called "Mother," lived just next door. We went over to say hello and meet her. She received us with open arms and offered us a snack. From all appearances, things were looking pretty good. I began to feel more at ease with every passing moment.

Lyden, situated on the west bank of the Demerara River, was a small community comprised of a few families. Wooden houses were on either side of the river. Varying distances separated individual houses, and there were either shrubs or fruit trees on the land between the houses. The main means of transportation was by small boats called *balaoos* or dugouts, which are commonly called canoes. I learned quickly that using a *balaoo* or canoe required some degree of skill. The terminologies used were strange to me at first, but over time, I learned what most of them meant.

In our yard there were two guava trees as well as a papaw tree. These fruit trees seemed to bear fruit year-round.

I was fascinated by the flow of the water in the river. At some times the tide flowed up river while at other times it flowed down river. At some periods during the month, the river water would rise higher than normal and overflow its banks, bringing with it debris and a variety of fish onto the land. Most of the houses in the village were raised several feet above the ground to prevent flooding whenever there was high tide. I particularly liked to bathe in the river when it was high tide. As I would dive into the water, a warm feeling would course through my body.

The main occupation in the village was farming. The farmlands were at the back of the houses. The villagers rose early in the mornings, prepared breakfast, and then left for the farm. Some farms were far away from the homes. Some villagers had to travel by boat to get to the farms. At the farms one could find a variety of vegetables, ground provision, bananas, and plantains being cultivated.

When new land was cleared for farming, the villagers used the slash and burn system for the most part. Once the land was cleared, cash crops were cultivated. These included a variety of vegetables and corn. Within three months of sowing, the corn was ready for reaping. I enjoyed corn either boiled or roasted. On selected evenings when corn was in season, families would light fires in their yards and roast corn. I enjoyed shedding ears of corn to their kernel and roasting them in the fire. At such times, the elderly would tell the children stories or riddles. This activity was enjoyed best on moonlit nights. The prevailing atmosphere and the cool temperatures made for memorable occasions.

It was at Lyden that I was introduced to secondary schooling. There was one school in the village that catered to children between the ages of 5 years 9 months and 18—some classes were combined. I settled into school nicely. While in school, I enjoyed science as well as literature and mathematics. I read avidly and would relate the stories to my stepmother at regular intervals. If there was an assigned textbook for my literature class, my stepmother would have me read a certain number of chapters per day and relate the story to her at nights. There was no way I could trick her into believing that I had read the assigned portion if I had not done so. On days when I did not take the book to school, she would read it during the day and quiz me when I got home from school. My stepmother also ensured that I put in a specified number of hours of study each evening after school.

Cousin Rachel also made sure that I learned how to take care of the home, from the preparation of my bed to the cooking of meals for the family.

On Saturday we cleaned the house as well as the yard. Every child in the home took a turn in this exercise. In the afternoon we baked bread and pastries at Mother's house. I was responsible for lighting the fire in the wooden oven, which was lined with metal on the inside to contain the heat. Even though there

Thy Will Be Done

was no way of baking at a fixed temperature, the finished product—bread or pastries—was mouth watering . The golden loaves of bread made your mouth water as the smell of freshly baked bread wafted through the air. The supplies lasted for as many as three or four days at a time.

During the week, after school let out for the day I helped Dad at his trade. As a shipwright, he built boats on the open space of land in front of our house. My brother and I were assigned a variety of tasks with varying degrees of difficulty or challenge. I cut wood, filled seams with putty after Dad caulked them with cotton or other material, and painted. Those were great learning opportunities. It was a pleasure to watch the boats take shape, be completed, and be eventually launched into the water at high tide.

As far as church attendance went, I would occasionally go with Mother to the Christian Brethren Church on Sundays. The church services were conducted by local elders from the community. At specified times during the year, the priest from the town of Linden, which was approximately thirty miles away, would visit and conduct special services. Whenever he came, these special services were planned over a period of several days. The night meetings were particularly well attended.

A favorite pastime in the community was cricket. The older men in the village would challenge teams from outside the village. At these matches, the women would prepare a variety of meals and most of the villagers would come out to support the team from the village. Apart from these special matches, the children in the village would play softball cricket regularly in their backyards or at school. I eventually developed a love for the game and blossomed into a fast bowler.

Without realizing it, I had settled in well to life with my stepmother and Dad.

***

At age 14, while still in attendance at Endeavour Christian Brethren School, I sat for the national Preliminary Certificate of Education Examination at the end of Form 3 (K 10). As I awaited the results of the PCE examinations, and with the advice and encouragement of the headmaster, Dad and my stepmother began to look for ways to have me complete secondary schooling since the school in the village did not tutor students beyond Form 3. Further, there was no school in the area that offered schooling beyond this grade. Consequently, the family had to look outside of the community for a suitable school.

Life in the Lyden Community

I overheard several late night conversations between my father and stepmother on the best possible choice of a high school for me to attend. Attempts were made to have me attend one of the secondary schools in Georgetown. However, because of my age, this proved difficult. Based on my age at that time, by the time I would be ready to sit for the General Certificate of Education (GCE) Examinations at the end of the fifth form, I would be too old to take the examinations.

I remember attending an interview at one school that was a good prospect only to be turned away because of my age. As I looked at other children dressed in their school uniforms and carrying textbooks around, I longed to be afforded such an opportunity. Dad kept up his search for a suitable school that I could attend.

One morning after Dad had returned from a trip to Georgetown, he told us over breakfast that during his trip he had met with one of my cousins who promised to seek out an opportunity for me to be able to attend school in Georgetown. Before long, news came through to Dad that I had been offered a place at the Trinity Methodist School in the city. This school offered classes up to Form 4 at which time students wrote the College of Preceptors (CP) high school equivalency external examination offered by the College of Preceptors of England. Qualifying at this exam gave a person the opportunity of either going on to secondary schooling up to the General Certificate of Education Examinations' Ordinary Level, depending on one's age, and then to the sixth form, which prepared students for the GCE Advanced Level Examinations. Success at the CP examinations was also a gateway to a teaching job with the Ministry of Education.

I welcomed this opportunity for further academic advancement and was beside myself with excitement at being able to attend school in the city. Because the school was a long distance from home, arrangements were made for me to stay with one of my relatives in the city.

I began school within a week of the offer from Trinity Methodist School. I stayed with my aunt in North Ruimveldt during the week and went home at least twice per month.

In the meantime, my father secured a piece of land at Long Creek on the Soesdyke Linden Highway where a major land development project was just starting up. Early on Sunday mornings we would journey to Long Creek as a family and work on developing the plot of land. The journey to Long Creek required traveling up river for approximately a mile, walking four miles through the forest, and then continuing another two miles along the Soesdyke Linden Highway. We would work late into the afternoon and then begin our trek back

Thy Will Be Done

home. The prospects of a "good life" at Long Creek kept the family returning there week after week.

After a while, because of this tiresome weekly exercise, my family began to give serious thought to relocating at Long Creek. After many family councils, it was decided that we all should move to Long Creek. This move would turn out to be a major turning point in my life.

Chapter 5

Relocation to Long Creek

The move to Long Creek took place in 1974. We moved there in stages. Each week one major set of household items and accessories were transported by river and road until almost all our belongings were moved. Dad had constructed a temporary shelter on the front portion of the 10-acre plot of agricultural land that he had acquired. The house was within close proximity to the main road.

When we moved to Long Creek, the Soesdyke-Linden Land Development Project (SLLDP) was in its early stages of development. Farmers were clearing their lands, either with the use of a bulldozer or manually. Roads and other landmarks in the village were being cut out according to the master plan for the development of the area. The community layout was completed in a few months.

I recall watching the bulldozer pushing back the forests as it uprooted trees and dumped them in piles at certain parts of the land. Fascinated at the entire process, I took an occasional ride or two on the rear of the bulldozer as it cleared the land.

Buildings were being constructed to house senior staff of the project. There was already a police station in the area. Homesteads began to go up on the plots of land that had already been fully or partially cleared.

The soil in the area was sandy with occasional red mud and clay mixed with sand and humus at some sections, particularly near the creeks. The latter kind of soil was fertile. New villagers kept moving to the area to take up residence and engage in farming.

At that time the Guyana government entered into an agreement with the Jamaican government to open up a massive emigrant scheme at selected villages along the Soesdyke Linden Highway. This involved the movement of Jamaicans who were residing in Britain at that time but were willing to move to Guyana with their families to work the land. This saw the arrival of many Jamaicans into the country.

Long Creek turned out to be the central point from which the SLLDP and the emigrant scheme were administered.

Thy Will Be Done

Many of the settlers at Long Creek had school-aged children. In time, the need for a school in the area became evident. Eventually, concerted efforts to have a school established got underway. While all these activities were going on in the community, I continued attending Trinity Methodist School.

A little under a year after my family moved to Long Creek, a decision was made that I should join them there and travel to school each day by bus some 34 miles away. I left home early in the mornings and returned late in the evenings.

The bus ride was enjoyable. I made new friends and did fun things on the bus. Going to school in the city and traveling by bus gave me a feeling of importance and excitement. While attending Trinity Methodist School, my love for literature was heightened. This was primarily because of my literature teacher who was well versed in literature and the arts. I was in the class that was preparing to write the College of Preceptors examinations, even though I did not sign up for the exam that year. The literature teacher read many of the plays, mostly Shakespearian, aloud, bringing the characters and scenes to life by the sheer skill with which she did the reading. The entire class was enthralled by the whole exercise and looked forward to her classes. Some of us even tried our hands at writing short plays and acting them out in class. I even wrote a poem for a special celebration and won first prize.

As I grew older, my interest gradually turned to the world of work. The cost of traveling to the city every day was becoming prohibitive for the family, so I decided to concentrate my efforts on helping Dad develop the farm.

By the end of 1974 the Ministry of Education had decided to start a school in the Long Creek community. This was to be a school for children aged 3 years 9 months to the late teens. The headmistress, Mrs. Joan Hinds, spread the news about the start up of the school and invited parents to enroll their children.

Since the enrollment included some older children, the headmistress explored the prospect of preparing those students to write the College of Preceptors Examinations through the school. She sought and obtained the necessary permission from the Ministry of Education to establish a class in the school for that purpose.

Even though passing remarks were made to me about enrolling at the school and joining this special class, I was not inclined to enroll in classes there because most of the other students were much younger than I was. I, therefore, spent a lot of my pastime during the day with the SLLDP Team, hoping to eventually secure an unskilled job with that project.

One morning while the men who worked with the SLLDP were gathered under their makeshift tent and carrying on their usual discussion on current issues, I interjected my interpretation of the subject under discussion. After I made my comment, one of the men asked, "Why aren't you going to school? You will do well in school." I muttered an excuse under my breath and eventually left the gathering without anyone noticing. Later that day, I told my parents about the conversation that I had had with the men earlier in the day. The passing remark made about my academic potential lingered in my memory.

Over the next several days after the discourse with the men at the SLLDP project site, I found myself thinking seriously about what had been said. I reasoned that since the opportunity to complete a few additional years of schooling was before me, and that I had nothing to lose but much too gain by so doing, the best course of action would be to return to school. I decided to swallow my pride and seek enrollment in the school if the headmistress would allow it at this late stage.

I discussed this prospect with my father and stepmother, and they were both in agreement with such a course of action. They even pledged to support me through school once I was accepted by the school's principal. Since my stepmother performed janitorial duties at the school, I asked her to approach the headmistress on my behalf regarding the possibility of the offer of a place in the secondary department.

One afternoon while performing her janitorial duties at the school, my stepmother broached the subject with the headmistress. When she returned home later that evening, she called me, "Alex,

"Yes, Cousin Rachael."

"Come, boy! I have some news to share with you about your intention to return to school."

"Coming in a minute!"

I left what I was doing and hurried to where she was sitting on the sofa in our living room and took a seat next to her.

"I just spoke to the headmistress about offering you a place in the secondary department of the school," she began.

"And what did she say?" I asked in a hurried tone.

"She actually said that it was okay."

"Thank you, Mum!"

I hugged and kissed her, my heart overflowing with gratitude.

"She wants to have a meeting with you tomorrow to discuss this further. There is no time to lose with this."

"Okay, I will go over to the school to meet with her first thing in the morning."

The next morning, I met with the headmistress in her office.

"Good morning, Alexander."

Thy Will Be Done

"Good morning, Miss."

"Your stepmother indicated to me yesterday evening that you would like to enroll as a student of this school."

"Yes, Miss. I would certainly like to take advantage of whatever additional schooling I can receive at this school."

"Alexander, I will be more than willing to have you as a student of this school. Of course, I will place you in the senior secondary department."

"Thank you, Miss!"

"You are a little older than the other students in the school, but do not let this fact bother you too much. Always keep in mind the reason why you are here, which is to complete your secondary schooling."

"I will give it my best shot."

"I will try to enroll a few other students in the senior secondary department. I can then prepare all of you for the CP examinations within a year if you are interested."

"I am certainly interested in such an arrangement. You can count me in."

"Your parents are respectable people in this community, and I would like to help you in whatever way I can, Alexander."

"Thank you so much, Miss."

"I will get back to you through your stepmother about the starting date for classes."

"Okay, Miss."

The golden opportunity for me to complete my formal schooling and acquire an academic qualification that would increase my prospects of landing a respectable job in the future had come, and I didn't let it pass me by. Moreover, I no longer had to contend with long hours of travel to and from school as was the case in the recent past.

One evening, not long after my meeting with Mrs. Hinds, my stepmother returned home from work and said, "Alex, I spoke to Mrs. Hinds this afternoon. She said that you can begin school in the morning." I was overjoyed.

I did not begin classes the following day since I had to get my school uniform and a few other needed items.

My dad gave me some money, and I went to Georgetown the following day and purchased my school uniform and the other needed items.

Since there was no time to lose, I began school the following day.

Chapter 6

In Touch With Adventism Again

Among the Jamaican families from England who settled at Long Creek was a Seventh-day Adventist family by the name of McIntyre. They lived on, and managed a poultry farm owned by a Seventh-day Adventist family who resided in the town of Linden.

John McIntyre and his wife, Sylvia, had two children attending school at Long Creek. Since there were a number of children who resided in the village, Mr. McIntyre decided to start up a Branch Sabbath School. He went from home to home and invited the children to the meetings, which were to be held under a small shed that he had constructed adjacent to his homestead.

He visited my home and invited us to Branch Sabbath School. My parents agreed, and I began attending with the other children from the village. Every Saturday afternoon Mr. McIntyre passed through the village with his car, picked up the children, and took us to Branch Sabbath School. At the end of the service, he took us back to our homes. The free car ride to and from the meetings was a good motivator to attend Branch Sabbath School.

I was glad for the opportunity to attend Branch Sabbath School once more. After attending Branch Sabbath School for a while, I got involved with the Pathfinder Club, and I completed several Pathfinder honors as a club member. Since regular church services were held on Saturdays, I began attending those as well. It did not take me long to integrate into the Seventh-day Adventist body of believers who fellowshipped at Long Creek each week. The novelty of reciting memory verses and completing Pathfinder honors lasted for a good while. And by studying the Bible each week, my knowledge of God increased.

Unfortunately, since attending church was not the "in thing" among young people in my community, attendance at church soon became a struggle for me. The lure of the world appeared appealing, and I began to entertain doubts about continuing to pursue a Christian way of life, especially since most of my friends were not following this way of life anyway. After a while, I began to attend services infrequently.

Thy Will Be Done

I remember expressing my doubts and uncertainty about continuing with church to a few of my friends who attended church with me. To my surprise, this got back to a few of the older members.

Sister Rogers, one of the senior members of the church, approached me one Saturday morning when I showed up for church. She was in her mid- to late-sixties, not more than five feet tall, and of medium built. Sister Rogers walked with a cane for support. She sat me down on the bench next to her, placed an arm around me, and began her speech. "Brother Alex, I am glad you came to church today. I missed you for a few weeks. I was really beginning to worry about you."

While I was still cowering from this unexpected personal encounter, she continued, "I heard that you are planning on not coming back to church. Is that so Alex?"

"I think I did say that to someone, but it was not meant to be taken as a conclusive statement."

"Is something bothering you, my dear?"

"Well, yes Sister Rogers. I feel a lot of pressure sticking with church when most of my close friends do not show any interest in practicing such a way of life. They tease me about my growing interest in the Christian way of life."

She brushed aside my remarks and continued, "Brother Alex, Jesus is one of the best friends you could ever have. And the Bible, His inspired Word, has the answers to all of life's questions. The Bible has some of the greatest love stories, historical accounts, and more. You name the subject, and it's mentioned in the Bible."

She had gotten my attention, and I was listening to her intently. "Jesus wants to be your best friend. If you make Him your best friend, your life will take on new meaning. So in spite of what your friends say, don't give up on Jesus now. Keep coming to church."

"I will think about it," I muttered.

"Alex, I want you to promise me that you will not give up on Jesus. Do I have your promise?"

"Er, er, ... yes, Sister Rogers."

What Sister Rogers said about Jesus and the Bible raised my curiosity. The Bible being presented as a book that could provide answers to all of life's questions was new knowledge for me. Before then I had not thought of the Bible in that way. Sister Rogers had given me food for thought. This changed my view about the Bible and its usefulness in dealing with real-life issues.

Within two years of their move to Long Creek, the McIntyres announced that they were returning to England. Their plan to settle in Guyana permanently

In Touch With Adventism Again

had not worked out as anticipated. The departure of the McIntyres opened up a job opportunity for someone to take over the thriving poultry business. Brother George Famey, a Seventh-day Adventist from the upper Demerara River, soon replaced the McIntyres as manager of the farm.

Brother Famey, "Georgie Porgie" as I fondly called him, moved to Long Creek with his family of fourteen. He was in his early fifties and of average height and medium built, but he hardly looked his age. He exuded an air of self-confidence and had a high self-esteem. Brother Famey was a devout Seventh-day Adventist Christian who took pains to command his household after him. A farmer for many years, he loved the outdoors. During the week he would leave home early in the mornings and return late in the evenings. He was dedicated to the work of the church and caring for his family.

With the arrival of the Famey family at Long Creek, the work of the Seventh-day Adventist Church in the village received a boost once more. Brother Famey and his family spearheaded the work of the Seventh-day Adventist Church in the village as best they could. He revived the Branch Sabbath School and sought to sustain it.

As far as I can remember, I stumbled on the family accidentally. While in conversation with Brother Famey, I was invited to church. I attended a few meetings and then did my best to evade his entreaties to continue. In fact, I hid whenever he passed through the village. However, because of his persistence, it was difficult avoiding him. I soon gave in to his many invitations and began attending church once more.

During this period I worked hard at my studies at Long Creek Government School in preparation for the College of Preceptors Examinations. I wrote the exams in July 1976, thus ending my formal years of schooling.

After finishing high school, I worked as an apprentice with a construction firm in the village while awaiting the results of my high school examinations.

When the examination results were released toward the end of the year, I was elated to learn that I had been successful. What I would be doing from that point on was unclear. To say the least, I was not inclined to continue with my apprenticeship. Since teaching was one of my career interests, I eyed a teaching job at my former school. If only I could secure a teaching job there, I would be off to a good start in life, I surmised.

In my own simple way, I prayed in earnest to God for guidance about my future life and work. I made a pact with Him. "Lord, if You help me to secure a teaching job," I prayed, "I will surrender my life to You in return and become one of Your followers."

To my surprise, my prayers were answered within a matter of weeks. The

Thy Will Be Done

head teacher of the school at Long Creek succeeded in securing a teaching job for me with the Ministry of Education, and on February 7, 1977, I began my teaching career at Long Creek Government School.

At that time the school was located in the Long Creek Compound. After the Guyana Defence Force (GDF) took over the Long Creek Compound a few years later, the school was subsequently moved to a new location about a mile away. The new school building was strategically located about twenty-nine miles from Georgetown, along the Soesdyke Linden Highway.

As you headed toward the school, you experienced a feeling of tranquility. The trees and the hills seemed to greet you. The first building along the road leading to the school was the head teacher's house. At the next corner on the left was the yellow one-story school building nestled among the trees of the forest.

Long Creek Government School was an example of an "all-age" school. On entering the building the first group of students you met was the preschoolers. This was followed by the elementary grades (1-6). Each grade was separated either by a screen or a blackboard. The classes were spread out in approximately equal portions of space. Toward the northern part of the building was a stage that accommodated the secondary department. To the right of the stage was the head teacher's office.

The yellow walls on the interior of the building were decorated with an assortment of teaching aids. Quotes such as "Time and Tide Wait on No Man" and "Quiet Speech is a Mark of Refinement" were written on cardboard and in the best hand.

I felt privileged to be on the teaching staff at the school. The head teacher, my parents, and some well-meaning community residents held out high expectations for me as a teacher and, therefore, encouraged me to give of my best in the execution of my duties. For my part, I embraced this golden opportunity to fulfill one of my career goals. I enjoyed my new job immensely and felt a sense of importance as a schoolteacher. I spared no pains to execute my duties in a highly competent and professional manner.

To my satisfaction and joy, my work met with great approval to the extent that community residents began to nudge me in the direction of advanced training in the teaching profession.

My devotion and love for God were heightened as a result of His answer to my prayer for a teaching job. My worship of God was now one of heartfelt gratitude. I stopped running from God, began attending church more frequently, and started to think seriously about His claims on my life. Since He had kept His part of the bargain, I resolved to keep my part.

Chapter 7

Conversion Experience

Within a few months of securing my teaching job, Brother Famey opened a Branch Sabbath School at Kairuni, a small predominantly Amer-Indian community approximately thirteen miles from Long Creek. The Kairuni group began meeting on Saturday afternoons, and over time, church services began to be held all day on Saturday. Gradually, most of the membership from the Long Creek Seventh-day Adventist Church transferred to Kairuni.

I traveled with the Fameys to those meetings and made some new friends. Several families traveled to church from as far as Silver Hill and Horadiah up to four or five miles away, while others came from the neighboring communities.

A special feature of the Saturday afternoon service at Kairuni was the convert's class, which was taught by Brother Wayland Ross, a distinguished local elder from the Peniel Seventh-day Church in Wismar, Linden. Every Saturday afternoon after lunch and a special time of relaxation and sharing, the Bible class convened. Brother Ross took us through topics such as repentance, conversion, new birth, the Word of God, the Law of God, baptism, justification, and sanctification. These were interspersed with some prophetic studies on the books of Daniel and the Revelation. Brother Ross' presentations kept us spellbound. He bridged the gap between the early Christian Church and the late twentieth century in an expert manner.

One prophetic application I vividly remember was this reference found in the book of Nahum, "The chariots shall rage in the streets, they shall justle one against another in the broad ways: they shall seem like torches, they shall run like the lightnings" (Nahum 2:4). Brother Ross likened the chariots to the motor vehicles of our day that ply our roadways. I was enthralled with these weekly presentations. The way Brother Ross delivered them conveyed to me that he was honest, knew his Bible well, had a good grasp of Bible prophecy, and had the gift of teaching.

As I attended the meetings each week, I felt the impressions of the Holy Spirit on my heart. The truths I was being exposed to were beginning to influence my concept of God and my outlook on life. I found myself beginning to dislike certain kinds of conversations, and I started associating more with

Thy Will Be Done

individuals who were of the Christian persuasion. I also began reading the Word of God with greater understanding, and Jesus Christ impressed on my mind the truths contained in His written letter to humanity. The words of the chorus of a song I knew—"The things I used to do, I'll do them no more"—became reality in my own experience.

Whenever there was a special convocation in the pastoral district that included Kairuni, I was invited to attend. I enjoyed the music and the preaching best. The sermons were presented in a dynamic and Spirit-filled manner while the music transported me to the heavenly realm. My love for Christ and His church began to take on added dimensions, and I knew that it was only a matter of time before the pull of the Holy Spirit would bring me over the line and enlist me in the ranks of Christ's followers.

Shortly after the thirteen solid weeks of Bible study under Brother Ross' tutelage, Brother Famey invited Pastor Lael Caesar of the Upper Demerara District to conduct a one-week reaping crusade at Kairuni. One evening on my way home from work, I ran into Brother Famey, and the following conversation took place.

"Brother Isaacs, I'm glad I saw you."

"What's up?"

"I would like to talk with you."

"Sure."

Knowing Brother Famey quite well, I braced myself for another engaging conversation about church and the Bible. He continued, "We are planning a one-week crusade at Kairuni beginning next Sunday, and I am extending to you a special invitation to the meetings. Pastor Lael Caesar will be the speaker."

While I was trying to absorb what he had just said, he went on, almost with the same breath, "I know that you will accept the invitation and get baptized at the end of the crusade."

I had heard Pastor Caesar preach before on at least two occasions, and I had been impressed with the scholarly and dynamic Spirit-filled messages he presented. I knew I would be in for a great spiritual experience by attending the meetings. I, therefore, had no difficulty accepting his invitation to the meetings.

On the other hand, even though I had been faithfully attending the Bible classes at Kairuni, I had not yet made up my mind about getting baptized. Brother Famey's indirect appeal to me about getting baptized at the end of the series put me on the spot.

Not wanting to appear disinterested in such a major decision in life, I responded to the invitation and the indirect call for baptism affirmatively. I looked forward to the nightly meetings with great expectancy.

Conversion Experience

During the week of the crusade, because of other preplanned activities, I was only able to attend meetings on Sunday, Wednesday, and Friday nights. When I showed up at the Friday evening service, everyone greeted me, including Pastor Caesar, who said, "Welcome, Brother Isaacs, we missed you. I was wondering if you had had a change of mind about your decision to follow Jesus all the way in baptism." I concluded then that Brother Famey had mentioned to him that I was a likely candidate for baptism.

Even though I had responded to Brother Famey in the affirmative earlier, not seeing me in attendance at the nightly meetings caused them to seem uncertain about my candidacy for baptism the following day. I reassured Pastor Caesar of my abiding interest in the meetings but could not attend every night because of prior commitments. Little did they know then that even though I could not attend nightly I had already made up my mind to be baptized at the end of the series. The messages were stirring, and the Holy Spirit convicted me of my need to stand for Christ.

During the Friday night meeting, I felt the impressions of the Holy Spirit encouraging me, more than ever before, to surrender my life to Jesus and get baptized. I could no longer resist the Holy Spirit's promptings. So, at the end of the service when Pastor Caesar made the appeal for persons to follow Jesus Christ into baptism, I went forward to the altar and surrendered my life to the Lord along with the others who had already gone forward. Pastor Caesar prayed for us and announced that the baptism would take place the following day.

When I returned home that night, I announced to my parents that I had made up my mind to follow Jesus and get baptized the next day.

On Saturday morning I awoke very early, had my devotion, and prepared for this major event in my life. Baptism by immersion had been emphasized and presented in an appealing way during the Bible classes. There was an allusion to the heavens opening and the Spirit of God descending in the form of a dove as it did when Jesus was baptized. I, therefore, eagerly looked forward to a Spirit-filled experience.

When I arrived at Kairuni on Saturday morning, there was excitement in the air. Individuals and families gathered for that day's special church service were looking forward to the baptismal ceremony with eager anticipation. The pews were filled.

The church service was impressive. One could have sensed the presence of the Holy Spirit among the gathering. We sang hymns of praise to God with fervor and meaning. It was as though the area had been invaded by the angels who sang at the birth of Jesus Christ. Some persons who were not in the building

Thy Will Be Done

peered out of their windows and some even joined in with the singing.

An Adventist male quartet from Linden had been specially invited to church at Kairuni that day. The quartet's renditions transported us to heavenly places. Other soloists were present and sang to God's name, honor, and glory in a similar manner. Pastor Lael Caesar preached the sermon with holy zeal. At the end of his sermon, he made a special appeal for individuals to surrender their lives to Jesus Christ and be baptized.

I went up to the altar as I had done the night before. There were some new people at the altar that morning who had not been there the previous night. A feeling of joy filled my heart. The baptismal vows were read, prayers were said, and then the minister led the way down to the edge of the Kairuni Creek to the baptismal site.

Trees and shrubs were on either side of the creek. At the edge of the creek, a spot of about six foot square had been cleared of shrubs and debris for the special occasion. The baptismal candidates put on baptismal robes over their clothes and stood on the banks of the creek awaiting the start of the service. The setting was one of tranquility.

It was high noon when the baptismal service began. Sunlight streamed down on the group. As if to offer some relief from the heat, clouds moved by slowly overhead, and some even appeared to remain motionless for a while in order to hide the gathering from direct exposure to the sun's rays. Occasionally, a cool breeze would pass over the area, cooling everyone down momentarily and, thus, making the heat more bearable.

I stared into the dark waters of the creek as it surged downstream. The water was inviting. Occasionally, a fish would jump out of the water, somersault, and land back into the water as if oblivious of our presence. As I stood there, my mind went back to the account of Jesus' baptism in the waters of the River Jordan as recorded in the Gospels.

Pastor Caesar waded into the water, parting it with his hands and testing its temperature as he did so. A surprised look crossed his face as he waded further out. The expression on his face and the cautious manner in which he proceeded seemed to convey an element of surprise at the coldness of the creek water even though the sun was shining brightly overhead. Standing in the water shivering somewhat, he prayed for God's presence and protection before proceeding with the baptismal service. The gathering sang choruses such as "I have decided to follow Jesus" and "Take me to the waters to be baptized." Passers by on the bridge above, attracted by the singing and the gathering below, stopped and glanced down at the proceedings. Some even lingered on for a while to take a closer look at the baptismal service.

Conversion Experience

The candidates then entered the water one after the other and were baptized by Pastor Lael Caesar. During the interval between each act of baptism, stanzas of particular hymns were sung and other musical scores wafted through the air. As the candidates came up out of the water, their faces were lit up and some of them praised God openly. Friends, relatives, and well-wishers congratulated them.

When my turn came to be baptized, I walked slowly toward the edge of the water, tested its temperature with my hands and then my feet, before going out to meet Pastor Caesar. As he took hold of my hands and guided me closer to where he was standing, I mused in my heart that this was the moment in my life I had looked forward to all along. When he submerged my body in the water and performed the act of baptism, I felt a sudden surge of joy and delight in my heart. When he brought me up from under the water, he tapped me on the shoulder and, in a somber tone of voice said, "Be a minister for Jesus!" Right there in the water, I had an inkling that God had a special plan for my life. The quartet then sang the song, "Don't you let nobody turn you round, keep on to Galilee," followed by, "I've paid my vows to the Lord, and I will not turn back," which was another moving rendition. The words of the songs inspired me to faithfulness in my walk with Jesus Christ from that point onward. The words, "Be a minister for Jesus," lingered in my memory as I made my way out of the water.

Once the baptismal service was over, the gathering returned to the tent. Over lunch there was much chatter as the gathering reflected on the events of the day. The faces of the newly baptized believers glowed with joy and delight in God. A feeling of satisfaction pervaded my being, and I could hardly wait to begin active Christian service.

At 3:00 p.m. a special service was convened. The new believers were congratulated and officially accepted into the fellowship of believers. Each one of the new converts was given a baptismal certificate and a copy of the devotional classic *Steps to Christ* by Ellen White. The remainder of the afternoon's program was in the form of a musical extravaganza. The quartet sang several pieces. Soloists, including the new converts, did the same. Those special renditions touched me to the core of my being. I had not experienced such joy before. I left church that day with such an overflowing joy that church members could not help but remark that God had done something wonderful for me. The sentiments of the day would long be remembered even after I ventured out on my newfound Christian experience.

Chapter 8

In Service for the Lord

My baptism marked a significant turning point in my life. With God as my Guide, my life took on a new sense of direction and purpose. I got to work immediately for the cause of Christ. I was appointed Sabbath School teacher for the youth class. Teaching that class provided me with an opportunity to influence the lives of the youth in a positive way. As time went by I became an elder-in-training and one of the teachers in the adult Sabbath School.

The rapidity with which I advanced in the church and the successes achieved encouraged me and gave me the impetus to continue expanding my role therein. Brother Famey led an ongoing outreach program to the Kairuni, Silver Hill, and Horadiah communities. This involved Saturday and Sunday afternoon visits to the homes of the church members and other community residents. Sometimes these visits involved walking for several miles. Because of problems with the public transportation system, walking was the only reliable means of getting from one point to the other. These visitation programs served as a viable means of keeping in touch with the membership and attracting and inviting new interests to the church.

As I accompanied Brother Famey and others on those trips, he would say to me, "Brother Isaacs, you are being trained now for your role as a pastor later on. This is the kind of work you will be involved in when you become a pastor. I am taking you through the paces now so that when the time comes you will know what to do."

As he spoke, there was a sense of seriousness and genuineness in his tone. As someone who had worked closely with many pastors before, and as an evangelist in his own right, Brother Famey had developed a knack for conducting successful home visitations, which he pursued aggressively.

Another important aspect of my early involvement in the work of the church was participating in crusades held at Horadiah and Silver Hill, respectively. These meetings required traveling as many as six miles inland from the Soesdyke Linden Highway, which sometimes included travel by boat. To encourage the residents in the community to attend the meetings, river transportation was provided. Before the start of the crusade each night, the boats went upstream and downstream and transported people to the crusade site. After the meetings, the boats took many of the attendees home. Once the people were safe in their homes, the crusade team, which comprised mostly of members who lived at Long Creek, began our homeward trek through the forest to the highway.

On the return journey, which began at approximately 10:00 p.m. each night, visibility was limited. This became more acute when it rained. I remember, on more than one occasion, it was difficult to see ahead for more than a few inches in any given direction because of rain, which made for poor visibility. Consequently, along the way, our heads occasionally collided with each other. In the darkness, you would hear, "Ouch!", followed by groaning as the affected members of the team held their heads and massaged the spot that hurt. After a collision, the pace slowed somewhat, and we continued on our journey more cautiously than before. I remember walking with my hands outstretched just above my shoulders in an attempt to avoid another collision in the dense darkness.

On a number of occasions, especially on rainy nights, the team was forced to stop moving in the darkness as we surveyed the road to decide which way to turn so that we would not take the wrong road. When it seemed that we could not advance any further with surety, a short burst of lightening would illuminate our path and point out the road ahead. The party would then move forward again.

On most nights by the time we got out to the highway the last bus from Linden, which took us home, had already passed. In those instances, the team chose either to walk until we were able to hitch a ride on a truck, tractor, jeep, or some other means of road transportation or wait it out for the rest of the night at Silver Hill until the following morning. In the latter case, we slept along the roadside or in the bus shed. On those occasions, to my dismay, many of the passengers on the bus that I would board the following morning were children whom I taught at Long Creek Government school. Therefore, once the bus dropped me off at the entrance to my home, I had to hurry inside, take a quick bath, have a hurried breakfast, and then rush off to my teaching job.

In spite of these challenges, I enjoyed what I was doing and consoled myself that this situation would not continue perpetually. I was happy to be serving God.

While on one of our outreach activities at Horadiah, I was given the opportunity to preach my first sermon. I took that assignment seriously and prepared for the event as best I could. Once I got in front of the audience, I preached with all the enthusiasm I could muster. As I spoke, the audience listened intently and punctuated the sermon with many "amens" and "hallelujahs," which encouraged me along.

After the sermon, Brother Famey took me aside and commended me for the presentation. He then gave a constructive critique on my sermon, being sure to point out areas of strength as well as weakness that could be improved upon. After that first sermon, I was increasingly afforded further opportunities to preach within my local congregation and elsewhere.

The gathering at Kairuni grew to the point that the temporary building where the meetings were held could no longer accommodate the group. There was need, therefore, for the group to seek out a bigger meeting area. With the consensus of the membership, a decision was made to abandon our makeshift meeting place at Kairuni and occupy a vacant building belonging to the Soesdyke Linden Land Development Project at Silver Hill, which was about half a mile away. This building was offered to us after we met with the authorities and explained our need. The group thus moved to Silver Hill.

Within a year or so of our move to the new meeting site, it became evident that a larger building was once again needed to house the group. The SLLDP administration was approached once more. Negotiations were made for a piece of land on which a new church could be erected. A short while after making the request to the local authorities, an acre of land was assigned for the construction of our new church.

By this time, I had become entrenched in the work of the church. My leadership skills were noted, and the church soon appointed me as an elder. This position gave me further exposure to the operations of the church. Concurrently, with my position as an elder, I served in most of the other departments of the church one time or the other. As I grew in grace and knowledge of Jesus Christ, the church soon gave me added responsibility by electing me as the first elder, the highest office a member could hold at the local Seventh-day Adventist Church.

Working in close collaboration with the District Elders Council of the Upper Demerara District, plans were laid for the construction of the new church building at Silver Hill. It was decided that construction of the church would be done by the members.

In addition to the members of the Silver Hill Church, the members of the District Elders Council traveled to Silver Hill early on Sunday mornings and joined with the church membership in the construction of the new building. On most Sundays the team worked well into the night. The church provided meals for the team. Occasionally, because of the unreliable nature of the road transporation system, Brother Famey and I traveled back to Silver Hill on

Saturday nights in order to be at the building site when the first set of workers from Linden arrived on Sunday morning.

Work on the new building moved apace. There was a high degree of motivation among the church members. Our plan was to complete the structure in as short a time as possible. The membership of the church gave sacrificially of their time and means. This, coupled with the ardent support from the other brethren from Linden, the generosity of community residents, and the Lord's providential workings, saw the new church building being completed in record time. The building was officially opened in 1984 to God's honor and praise. This was a signal achievement for everyone involved. It was a joyous occasion to actually worship in our own building. I was ordained as a local elder that same year.

During my tenure as elder, I conducted several lay crusades in the Silver Hill and Long Creek communities, and I was overjoyed to see several individuals join the church. Concurrently, I was given ample opportunity to sharpen my preaching skills by way of preaching appointments at sister churches within the Upper Demerara District. Based on the feedback received and their willingness to schedule me for preaching appointments, it was evident that my preaching was getting across to the believers. This gave me a sense of accomplishment and motivated me to continue giving of my best in service to the Lord.

I found the combination of my work as a teacher and a church leader rather unique and enjoyable. One seemed to complement the other, and I marveled at how the Lord blessed my efforts for Him.

As I matured in the work of the Lord, I began to consider becoming a full-time gospel worker. From all indications, this was the direction in which God was leading. However, I wanted to be sure that my ambition to become a minister was what God intended for me. I, therefore, sought to find out what was God's will in that regard.

Chapter 9

Holy Spirit: Faithful Guide

Very early in my Christian life, I experienced first-hand, a manifestation of God's guiding hand in my life. One day I went into the forest to cut down trees to use for the production of charcoal. Before commencing work, I placed my spectacles safely behind a partly decayed log. By 5:00 p.m., I had completed a satisfactory day's work, so I decided to return home for the night.

Just around nightfall, after I had eaten supper, I decided to immerse myself in a good book. But when I reached for my spectacles, they were not in their usual place. I realized then that I had not brought them home from the forest, so I immediately went to retrieve them.

By the time I reached the spot where I had placed my spectacles, it was already dark. I reached down behind the log with my right hand and groped for them in the darkness. But all I could feel were dead leaves and twigs. I began to feel uneasy, so I took another quick swipe behind the log, this time with both hands. The result was the same. Thinking then that I had probably made a mistake regarding the exact location of my spectacles, I searched frantically along the full length of the log, as well as the surrounding area. My spectacles were nowhere to be found!

When I returned home that night, I told my family what had happened. They scolded me. One of them sarcastically said, "Now we will see if God will help you find your spectacles." He went on further in a somber tone, "You can't get those spectacles back. You will have to buy a new pair."

I could not bear the thought of losing my spectacles at that time. They were prescription spectacles, and I relied on them heavily because of the volume of reading which I had to undertake. Personally, I could not afford the money to purchase another pair. My salary was very small, and I did not have any savings for such an expense. In addition, my family was not in a position to help me either. I, therefore, had to find my spectacles.

I presented my problem to God in prayer. Drawing encouragement from Bible promises and instances of God's divine intervention in the lives of people, I believed that somehow He would help me find my spectacles and at the same time vindicate His name. Ephesians 3:20 became especially relevant: "Now

Holy Spirit: Faithful Guide

unto him that is able to do exceeding abundantly above all that we may ask or think, according to the power that worketh in us."

That night I lay awake in bed longer than usual. My thoughts were preoccupied with the happenings earlier in the day and what approach I should take in trying to recover my spectacles. While I was talking to God about the problem, the Holy Spirit impressed forcibly on my mind that someone had picked up my spectacles from behind the log. But who could have possibly done so? By the process of elimination, one name stood out—Mr. Bhudia, a wood cutter who lived on the edge of the forest about three miles inland from the main road. However, there were other people I thought of who could have picked them up. I was, therefore, in a quandary trying to ascertain who had picked them up. I kept the matter before God in prayer.

As I continued to pray about the situation, the Holy Spirit impressed on my mind again that Mr. Bhudia was the one who had picked up my spectacles. So I decided to go to his home the following morning to recover them. Unfortunately, getting there posed a major challenge because I did not know the way to his house. As I did not want to disclose my peculiar problem to anyone else by asking for directions, I turned to the Holy Spirit for guidance.

During my personal devotions the next morning, I stumbled on Isaiah 30:21: "And thine ears shall hear a word behind thee, saying, This is the way, walk ye in it, when ye turn to the right hand, and when you turn to the left." Because of my current circumstances, I embraced this Bible promise with all my heart.

Venturing into the forest so early in the morning was fraught with danger. If I went in the wrong direction, I could easily get lost or run into wild animals. Therefore, before leaving home for Mr. Bhudia's residence, I prayed earnestly for God's protection and the Holy Spirit's guidance during my journey.

I set out for Mr Bhudia's residence just about the break of dawn. The path to his home passed through the portion of land on which I had worked the previous day.

As I made my way through the forest, the cool morning air wafted over my face and hands, producing a feeling of tranquility. The birds had already begun singing their morning praises to God. The varied melodies filled the atmosphere with music. The dew that had accumulated on the leaves of the trees changed gradually into water droplets that burst and fell to the ground. Occasionally, some water droplets from the overarching trees burst and bathed my face and hands. A squirrel scuttled across my path, causing me to stop abruptly before continuing on my journey.

At various points along the way, I came upon crossroads. As I approached them, I would slow my pace and study them in order to decide in which direction I should go. In those instances, I prayed, "Lord, please guide me in the right path." The Holy Spirit then pointed the way forward.

On one occasion I ventured through a track that turned out to be a roundabout. I believe strongly that that was the Lord's way of leading me away from some danger that was lurking in my path. After walking for approximately thirty-five minutes, I began noticing signs of recent human activity. In one place several trees and underbrush had been freshly cut. Further on there was a half-filled bottle of gasoline partly visible from behind a freshly cut tree stump at the side of the road.

As I continued my journey, my thoughts were preoccupied with how I would approach Mr. Bhudia. Should I tell him that I had a notion that he had picked up my spectacles from the forest? Or, acting on the Holy Spirit's impressions, should I tell him outright that yesterday afternoon someone picked up my spectacles from behind a log in the forest and that God, through His Holy Spirit, had revealed to me that he, Mr. Bhudia, was the one who had done so?

The trail eventually led to a junction. Unsure of which way to turn, I stopped and surveyed the area, trying to decide which direction would lead to Mr. Bhudia's house. Going left, I would have to pass through a deep, dark ravine. Going right, I would be able to see clearly ahead for about one hundred yards at which point the road tended downhill.

My inclination was to turn right. However, to be sure, I turned to God in prayer and asked Him to point me in the right direction. No sooner had I prayed than the "still small voice" of the Holy Spirit impressed me to take the road to the left.

As I picked my way through the ravine, I kept on the alert. Stumbling onto someone so early in the morning could cause that person's self-protection instincts to kick in and either party could get hurt or even be killed.

The track through the ravine seemed unending. After walking for about twenty-five yards, my pace slowed considerably. I was beginning to wonder if I was actually on the right track. Just then a rooster crowed loudly in the distance. With this indication that I was nearing civilization, I stepped up my pace once more and headed in the direction from which the sound was heard.

The path soon led downhill. As I began my descent, I saw a man approaching with his head faced downwards. He was carrying a shotgun in one hand and a cutlass in the other. As he came closer, I recognized that it was Mr. Bhudia. This was my moment of truth!

I stopped and observed him closely. When he was within earshot, I called out in a friendly tone, "Good morning, Mr. Bhudia."

Startled at the sound of my voice, he paused momentarily and raised his head. A puzzled look crossed his face. But when he realized it was me, he gave a half-smile and said, "Morning, Isaacs. What has brought you here so early?"

I got straight to the point. "Yesterday while working out front, I hid my spectacles behind a log and forgot them there. Later in the evening when I found them missing, I returned to the forest to retrieve them, but they were gone!" As I spoke, there was an intrigued look on his face. I continued, "God, through His Holy Spirit, revealed to me that *you* picked up my spectacles. I have, therefore, come to retrieve them."

His countenance did not show any signs of concurrence with what I was saying. My heart sank. Had I been misled? Maybe I had been wrong all along about God's guiding hand in this whole exercise. I looked away briefly.

When I regained eye contact with Mr. Bhudia, his face wore a cunning smile. Then he began, "God must have spoken to you, indeed, because yesterday evening, while on my way home from Georgetown, I stumbled upon a pair of spectacles. I reasoned that someone had probably dropped them by accident, so I picked them up with the intention of taking them out to the village later today in case someone may have reported them missing."

He continued, "The spectacles are at my house. Go down to the house and tell my wife to give them to you. They are on the shelf in the kitchen."

I thanked Mr. Bhudia and hurried down to his bungalow at the bottom of the hill while he continued on his journey. When I got to the house, I greeted his wife and explained to her what had happened. When I was through talking, she went into the house and came back several seconds later carrying a pair of spectacles in her hands. After she handed them to me, I opened the carrying case, examined them, and found that they were mine indeed! I thanked her and left.

As I made my way home, my heart was overflowing with gratitude to God. I stopped in my tracks, knelt down, bowed my head, and thanked Him for helping me find my spectacles. Right there in the forest, on my knees, I promised to be faithful to Him for the rest of my life because of this experience. In my excitement, I held my spectacles securely and ran all the way home, eager to share the good news with my family.

I made it home in less than half the time it took me to get to Mr. Bhudia's house. My energies were spent, but I was elated. God, through His Holy Spirit, had wrought good things in my behalf, and I was overjoyed.

As I recounted the happenings of the morning to my family, everyone was filled with wonder and amazement at God's intervention. They in turn expressed thanks to God. They had never seen it in such a fashion. Neither had I. Everyone concurred with me that indeed God had delivered me out of a difficult and seemingly impossible life situation.

Thy Will Be Done

This encounter with God strengthened my faith and trust in Him, and it has impacted my life in many ways ever since.

Chapter 10

The Call to be a Pastor

The statement, "Be a minister for Jesus," which Pastor Caesar uttered at my baptism, was kept fresh in my mind. In an effort to gain a good understanding of what was involved in being a minister of the gospel, I observed closely the work of the pastor who served in the Upper Demerara District.

Whenever Pastor Caesar preached at Kairuni, I observed his use of diction, language, tone of voice, sincerity, and the passion with which he delivered his sermons. I got the feeling that he was sincere about what he was saying. His messages got across to his listening audience. Pastor Caesar seemed to enjoy his job and was always ready to attend to the needs of the flock. Anyone who associated with him got the feeling that he was someone who lived close to God. To this day, many of the brethren reminisce on the good times they shared with Pastor Caesar while he served in the Upper Demerara District.

One of Pastor Caesar's strong points, as highlighted by the membership, was his house-to-house visitation with members. During those visits, he listened to them, encouraged them, gave advice, and prayed with them. This made his sermons more real-to-life and focused as he sought to speak to the needs of his parishioners. He earned the respect of the brethren and was seen as a caring pastor.

One day while I was at the Linden Car Park in Georgetown awaiting transportation to travel to Long Creek, Pastor Caesar showed up and struck up a conversation. At one point during our discourse, he asked about my academic standing. After hearing my response, he said, "You should apply to Caribbean Union College [CUC] to study for the ministry. I believe you will do well there."

Pastor Caesar believed that I had the making of a minister. I was pleasantly surprised at his words and the genuineness with which he uttered them. I began to get the feeling that his pronouncement at my baptism, "Be a minister for Jesus," was more than just a passing statement. Rather, in my view, it was deliberate and inspirational.

Even though I had aspirations of attending Caribbean Union College in the future, I did not envision doing so that soon after my baptism. Nevertheless, working on the advice of Pastor Caesar, I wrote CUC and requested application materials. Even as I wrote the college, I knew that one of my major constraints would be finances to fund my studies.

In time Caribbean Union College replied to my letter and sent me an application package, which I promptly completed and returned to the college. Soon after submitting my application, the college wrote back, informing me that I was accepted into the bachelor of theology degree program.

In order to attend college, I had to secure the necessary financial assistance. From my end, funds were extremely scarce. I, therefore, explored several other sources of funding. One source that held much promise was the Guyana Conference of Seventh-day Adventists. At the opportune time, I resolved to bring up the matter with Pastor Roy I. McGarrell who was the president of the conference at that time.

Pastor McGarrell was about five-feet eleven-inches tall, well-built, and of African lineage. He carried himself with dignity. As one of the most outstanding and successful pastors who served in the Guyana Conference, he became president of the conference in 1976. As president, Pastor McGarrell gave the members a listening ear and was always willing to offer advice and guidance to those who sought him out. He was a dynamic preacher and held his audiences spellbound throughout his messages. Pastor McGarrell was well-loved and respected by the constituency. The opportunity to raise this matter with him was not long in coming.

One Saturday morning while on his way to Linden to speak at a district convention, Pastor McGarrell offered me a ride in his car. During the trip, we chatted on a variety of subjects. He eventually came around to the subject of my future academic and professional development plans. I disclosed to him my intentions to attend Caribbean Union College in preparation for entrance into the ministry. I told him that I had already been accepted to CUC but lacked the financial backing to be able to embark on my study program.

On learning of my interest in attending Caribbean Union College, Pastor McGarrell set up an appointment for me to meet with him at his office so that we could discuss the subject further.

I met with Pastor McGarrell at the time appointed, and we discussed my study plans at length. During the meeting, he pointed out some of the challenges of pastoral ministry as well as the solemn responsibilities that are inherent in the ministerial line of work. He encouraged me to follow through with my study plans.

Pastor McGarrell promised to explore the possibility of me receiving a partial tuition scholarship from the Guyana Conference to assist in funding my intended study program. He took the time to outline to me the obligations associated with the tuition scholarship award.

The Call to be a Pastor

"Even though you are not compelled to return to Guyana on account of receiving a tuition scholarship award, it will be a good gesture for you to come back to Guyana after you have completed your studies at CUC nonetheless, and give some service to the constituency. After all, it is the brethren's hard-earned money that will be used to fund the scholarship. By returning to Guyana and serving in the field, it will convey to the conference constituency your gratitude for being offered a tuition scholarship to study at CUC."

I assured him that I planned to return to Guyana after college and render service to the constituency.

The conference administration decided to offer me a tuition scholarship to study at Caribbean Union College. However, for some unknown reason, the decision was not communicated to me then. And since I had not secured any other financial assistance, I shelved the idea of entering Caribbean Union College for the time being. I communicated my decision to Pastor McGarrell by way of letter.

Pastor McGarrell expressed his disappointment at my decision not to follow through with my plans to attend college that year. It was then that I learned of the Conference Executive Committee's earlier action to offer me a tuition scholarship to study at CUC for that very year. Even though Pastor McGarrell wished that I had not changed my mind about attending CUC, he encouraged me not to abandon the prospect of attending CUC altogether. He left Guyana in 1980 to pursue advanced studies overseas.

At church several of the believers constantly encouraged me to train to enter the ministry as a pastor. Foremost among the members who encouraged me in this direction was Sister Greene, an elderly member from the McKenzie No. 1 Seventh-day Adventist Church, which was later renamed Emmanuel SDA Church, in the town of Linden.

Sister Greene was not more than five-feet tall. Bent over with age, this sweet old lady was a permanent fixture in her home church. During regular church services, she sat in the same seat, about four rows from the rear of the church on the right. Liked and respected by young and old alike, Sister Greene was always ready to offer a word of advice or encouragement to those who stopped by to greet her before, during, or after the church service.

Whenever Sister Greene spotted talent or potential for the advancement of God's kingdom, she encouraged its development to the hilt. Her magical words were, "I am praying for you." Sister Greene exuded an enthusiasm that was anchored in an unshakable faith in God and belief in His Word. Doing God's will and building up His kingdom were her all-consuming passion. She used every opportunity afforded her to share her faith. In short, her godly influence touched the lives of many.

Thy Will Be Done

I remember one Saturday morning just after I had finished preaching at the Emmanuel church that Sister Greene pulled me aside and said, "Brother Isaacs, you have a good preaching talent. You must enter Caribbean Union College and train to become a pastor." From that first admonition by Sister Greene, she kept repeating it to me whenever we had a chance to chat. I had to continually reassure her that even though I had not yet taken up her challenge in that regard, I had not abandoned the idea but planned to do so some time in the future.

Another prominent Christian believer who constantly urged me on in the direction of CUC and the ministry was Brother Famey. This servant of God had an eye out for potential, especially when related to the advancement of the kingdom of God. Wherever he spotted such potential, he sought to see that it was fully developed. He was anxious to see me enter CUC. As though speaking to me constantly on this subject was not enough, he communicated to my parents his thoughts on the subject. The way he conveyed this to my parents time and again served to eventually convince them that this was a worthwhile option.

Whenever it appeared to Brother Famey that I was not showing enough interest in, or making definite plans to enter Caribbean Union College, he would pull me aside and say, "Brother Isaacs, when will you be attending Caribbean Union College? If you keep on putting this thing off, you will eventually end up not going after all, and you will lose a great opportunity to train as a pastor. Son, you have to make up your mind and just go."

If I made the excuse that I did not have enough money to pay my way through college, he would say, "Listen to me; money is not a problem! God owns the cattle upon a thousand hills, and He can more than provide for *your* needs!"

I listened to what Brother Famey had to say, and I sought to reassure him time and again that I had not abandoned my plan to enter Caribbean Union College. The timing was just not right for me to do so. That served to somewhat quiet his fears that my mission to CUC had been abandoned altogether. Other members encouraged me along the same line, and I felt that God was speaking to me through the members' utterances and encouragement.

Since first encouraging me to apply to CUC to train to be a minister, Pastor Lael Caesar, up until the time of his departure for the United States to further his studies, constantly sought to persuade me to pursue that line of work. After Pastor Caesar's departure, Pastor Colin Parkinson replaced him as district pastor. Pastor Parkinson visited our church at Silver Hill on several occasions, and he asked me on more that one occasion when I would be attending CUC. I told him that I would be going there some day.

The Call to be a Pastor

In addition to other members of the church, my father and stepmother encouraged me to become a pastor. I believe that Dad's motivation was fueled to some extent by what Brother Famey and other individuals had told him about the special privilege of having a son who was a minister. Moreover, on innumerable occasions, Dad reminisced about his early years in the Moravian Church when he served as an altar boy. Probably spotting the potential for one of his sons to attain to a higher church office than that at which he had served as a young man, Dad declared to me in no uncertain terms that he would not at all mind me studying for the ministry. "I will feel honored to have a son who is a pastor," he would say from time to time.

My stepmother shared and expressed similar sentiments and was also a constant source of encouragement in this regard. In her eyes, becoming a pastor would be a signal achievement.

Although I was unable to attend college at that time, I diligently worked in the community and its environs. My efforts at fostering the work of the church at Silver Hill were blessed with success after success. Moreover, I enjoyed working in the building up of God's church. I took the Lord's work seriously. Whenever, I was to be engaged in some line of work for God, I took the pains to plan as thoroughly as I could. This approach was most pronounced when it was time for preaching at some lay crusades.

I went over the biographies of some of the world's greatest preachers. I read about one particular preacher from London who practiced his sermons in his cathedral during the day in preparation for his nightly meetings. On one occasion, the preacher recounted that while practicing his sermon, a carpenter perched on some scaffolding doing some repair work on the interior of the cathedral began to listen to the minister as he rehearsed his sermon. As the sermon progressed, the preacher observed that the hammering became less frequent. By the time of the appeal, the hammering had stopped altogether. As the preacher made the altar call, to his surprise, the carpenter laid down his hammer, climbed down the scaffolding, made his way to the altar in tears, and surrendered his life to Jesus Christ.

Taking a page out of that preacher's book as it were, I prepared for the lay crusades as thoroughly as possible. Each morning before leaving for work, I retired to the forest at the back of our house and set up a makeshift pulpit on one of the tree stumps. There, I would practice my sermon from start to finish, taking care to carry out the appeal in the process. On other occasions, I would practice my preaching skills on my way to school along the track through the forest. By so doing, I soon discovered that my preaching was much more convincing and flowed better during delivery.

Thy Will Be Done

I remembered one year, during the Christmas season, the ministerial students from Caribbean Union College visited Guyana while they were on break and preached at the area churches during the Sabbath services. In the afternoons all the ministerial students converged at one church and shared their experiences with the membership who came from across the district. As I listened to the students talk about their experiences at college and observed their preaching abilities, I longed to attend CUC to be trained as a minister. After all, attending CUC was making a difference in the lives of these students, and I desired a similar experience.

While Pastor K. Eugene Ford, education director of the Caribbean Union Conference of Seventh-day Adventists, was on one of his visits to Guyana, I discussed my career projections with him and asked for some advice and guidance on the subject. Taking into consideration my aptitude for science and my perceived call to the ministry, he advised that I endeavor to enter the medical profession and simultaneously pursue theological studies. Pastor Ford pointed out that such a combination of disciplines would help me make maximum use of my academic acumen, noting that a medical career blends itself well with pastoral ministry.

As I began to give serious thought about attending CUC, I kept in mind Pastor Ford's suggestion, resolving to seek out opportunities at CUC whereby I could pursue training in health or medicine and theology concurrently.

In my quiet moments, I reflected on all the happenings in my life up to that point. God seemed to be pointing me in the direction of pastoral ministry. However, I wanted to be sure that this was His will for my life before immersing myself into this vocation.

Chapter 11

Sorting Out the Call

My teaching stint at Long Creek Government School was turning out to be a rather enjoyable and fruitful encounter. I liked it so much that I hoped to someday undergo specialized training in an educational field. If circumstances permitted, I wanted to pursue a degree in teaching. However, at the same time, my desire to pursue training in pastoral ministry at CUC did not subside; rather, it grew stronger. I, therefore, struggled to decide which way to go.

To help me make up my mind about God's will for my life, I utilized a variety of approaches.

First, I made this subject a matter of constant prayer. I was mindful of the usefulness of prayer in attempting to find out God's will for one's life. From my study of literature, I had come across this quote from Alfred Lord Tennyson: "More things are wrought by prayer than this world dreams of." This statement took on new meaning and importance during this critical period of my life.

Biblical statements about prayer and its power became a source of encouragement and guidance in the process. Texts such as the following sustained my faith and kept me pushing forward:

"Praying always with all prayer and supplication in the Spirit, and watching thereunto with all perseverance and supplication" (Eph. 6:18).

"Be careful for nothing; but in every thing by prayer and supplication with thanksgiving let your requests be made known unto God" (Phil. 4:6).

"… men ought always to pray, and not to faint" (Luke 18:1).

"Pray without ceasing" (1 Thess. 5:17).

I also dedicated one day each week solely to prayer and fasting. During those sessions, I poured out my soul to God as I sought His will for my life.

Along with prayer and fasting, I diligently studied my Bible. In so doing, I came across many passages of scripture that gave me comfort and hope.

"For this God is our God for ever and ever: he will be our guide even unto death" (Ps. 48:14).

"A man's heart desireth his way: but the Lord directeth his steps" (Prov. 16:9).

"Thy word is a lamp unto my feet, and a light unto my path" (Ps. 119:105).

"I will instruct thee and teach thee in the way which thou shalt go: I will

Thy Will Be Done

guide thee with mine eyes" (Ps. 32:8).

"Nevertheless I am continually with thee: thou hast holden me by my right hand. Thou shalt guide me with thy counsel, and afterward receive me to glory" (Ps. 73:23, 24).

"And the Lord shall guide thee continually" (Isa. 58:11).

"Thus saith the Lord, thy Redeemer, the Holy One of Israel; I am the Lord thy God which teacheth thee to profit, which leadeth thee by the way that thou shouldest go" (Isa. 48:17).

"Trust in the Lord with all thine heart; and lean not unto thine own understanding. In all thy ways acknowledge him, and he shall direct thy paths" (Prov. 3:5, 6).

"The steps of a good man are ordered of the Lord: and he delighteth in his way" (Ps. 37:23).

I also relied on the Holy Spirit for guidance. This inspirational verse of Scripture about the guidance of the Holy Spirit found in Isaiah 30:21 was very helpful: "And thine ears shall hear a word behind thee, saying, This is the way, walk ye in it, when ye turn to the right hand, and when ye turn to the left."

My quest for direction in regards to my choice of a career took me down other paths. I immersed myself in focused research on the subject of "the call to the Gospel ministry."

During my research, I came across the following statement on page 43 of the Caribbean Union College 1977-79 Bulletin: "The sacred ministry is a divine calling that should be entered into advisedly with adequate consideration for the demand and the responsibility involved in its pursuit. If at any time during a student's training, it becomes apparent that his spirituality, scholarship, or conduct does not relate to the high standard of the ministry, it is advisable for him to discontinue the theology course."

As I reflected on this statement, I inferred several things. First, a minister of the Gospel is called of God. Therefore, God is the One who should give the marching orders. Second, one's decision to enter the sacred ministry should not be made hastily. By extension, such a decision should not be based solely on the fact that others are doing so, that the sacred ministry brings prestige and respect with it, that the minister has the potential of being in a position of authority, or that it just feels good being a minister of the Gospel. As good as those reasons might be in and of themselves, they do not constitute sufficient grounds for entering the ministry. Third, the statement was inferring that godly advice should be sought. Fourth, the individual must carefully consider the demands and duties involved in ministry. Fifth, it became clear to me that ministers are expected to uphold a very high standard of Christian conduct.

Sorting Out the Call

In summary, I viewed the ministry as serious business and a vocation that should not be trifled with.

I had all these thoughts running through my mind when I studied the sermon "The Divine Imperative" by Pastor Nembahard of the Inter-American Division of Seventh-day Adventists. After reading the sermon, I felt as though the Lord was calling me to the ministry.

However, I craved further advice on the subject before coming to a definite decision. That day, I wrote in my diary the following entry:

> On certain occasions there is a burning desire to answer the call to the ministry. I humbly submit that the qualities, from a human standpoint, and traits necessary for successfully serving in the ministry have been demonstrated by me. My only requirement now is a direct, personal call to me from heaven. I am entreating the Lord to grant me same in His own way. What is needed is a clear, unmarred call from God. I am prepared to listen to the Lord's voice as He speaks to my conscience. Need the divine revelation. The Lord's will be done.

I declared June 12 a day of prayer and fasting in order to discover the Lord's will in the matter of my call to the ministry.

The following day I decided to approach Elder Gordon Martinborough, president of the Guyana Conference of Seventh-day Adventists, for advice on how I could be certain, from a heavenly perspective, whether or not the Lord had indeed called me to be a pastor. However, on arrival at Elder Martinborough's office I discovered that he was out of the country. I attempted to speak with other senior ministers who were around, but I was unable to set up a meeting with them. I felt somewhat dejected at that time.

I resorted to the stance of waiting on the Lord for His will to be revealed in this very important matter.

As time went by I continued to feel a compelling urge to enter the ministry. I had already received a lot of encouragement from church members, friends, and others, including my parents, to take up the ministry. Those admonitions became more pronounced. The popular statement in Christian circles that, "The voice of the people is the voice of God," came to mind then.

As I wrestled with the option of entering the ministry, I began to have dreams about preaching. These dreams occurred occasionally at first but became more frequent with the passage of time. An entry from my diary dated

Thy Will Be Done

March 1985 read, "Had a dream that found me preaching to a large crowd of interested people. I was expounding on a portion of Scripture and the Holy Spirit gave me utterance concerning the text's exposition. Don't know if the Lord is calling me to the Gospel ministry."

During the next few months, I had several similar dreams to the one in March. In one of those dreams, I found myself among a group of ministers of the Guyana Conference of Seventh-day Adventists meeting the needs of the people. At one point in the dream, I was in attendance at a training workshop in Georgetown, which was sponsored by the Guyana Conference of Seventh-day Adventists. In the dream Elder Martinborough lectured on effective methods of evangelism.

Similar dreams occurred with increasing frequency. In a dream received on May 4, I found myself conducting an evangelistic campaign at the Silver Hill SDA Church. The crowd that had gathered seemed quite enthusiastic, and the messages were well received.

Four days later I had another dream. This time I was engaged in a weekend camp meeting at which church members from all parts of Guyana were in attendance. In my dream I played an integral part in the conducting of the workshop. This was followed by another dream the following night. In that dream I was involved in another camp meeting, and again, I participated meaningfully.

Very early on the morning of June 27 of that same year, I wrote in my diary: "Had another dream tonight. First, I was at some church function, and Pastor Winston Patterson was the officiating pastor. He strongly advised me to take up the gospel ministry, saying that it was the Lord's will that I should enter same."

I mentioned this dream to my stepmother, and she surmised that it might well be the Lord calling me to the ministry after all.

Later that day I visited the Guyana Conference office and spoke with a senior pastor. During our discourse I mentioned to him my interest in joining the ministry. He advised that I enter Caribbean Union College and pursue theological training there. The pastor disclosed to me, in a solemn manner, that he had high regard for men of courage and that I should apply to Caribbean Union College, emphasizing that CUC was among the best schools of theological training in the Caribbean. It was dubbed "The School of the Prophets." The pastor offered his assistance in helping me secure the required application form. He further offered to submit the application to the college on my behalf.

We were subsequently joined by a few other ministers, and by the end of my discussion with the pastors, I felt that the Lord was indeed calling me to the ministry. The tone of the conversation seemed to suggest that there was no time to lose in entering Caribbean Union College. However, I still persisted in my

Sorting Out the Call

quest for further advice on the subject. I wanted to at least discuss the subject with the conference president and get his input before going any further.

I subsequently met with the conference president, Elder Gordon Martinborough, to discuss the subject.

During our discourse, I informed him of my inclination to enter the gospel ministry and the recent happenings in my life in that regard. He was candid in his discussion on this matter. The president pointed out, among other things, that the call to ministry is a personal matter. He shared with me the emerging landscape of the gospel ministry in the Caribbean Union and some of the challenges I was likely to face were I to pursue studies at CUC.

One of his main concerns was the funding of my education while at college. Students who wished to enter CUC then had to have sufficient funds to at least be able to pay for their first year's college expenses. My plan was to work part time on campus and seek out other sources of funding. For example, I had heard previously that the college had a program whereby a student would work full time on campus for one year to raise enough funds so that he or she could begin classes the following year. However, Elder Martinborough informed me that the program had been discontinued. He noted further that should I opt to pay my school fees with Guyanese dollars I would be faced with the problem of securing foreign exchange because of restrictions that had been recently imposed by the Bank of Guyana. Those restrictions would make it difficult for me to transfer funds to CUC or even secure foreign currency to take along with me. Therefore, from all appearances, my financial plan did not seem to add up.

According to the President, these were sobering concerns which I needed to think through. Then Pastor Martinborough interjected on a positive note, "In spite of these challenges, as an individual you have some positive traits for the ministry. You are a local church elder, and you have some experience leading out in the church…."

He concluded the discourse with, "Ask the Lord to reveal His will for your life in a more tangible way. Keep on the lookout for open doors." He then offered prayers on my behalf. Before leaving his office, I thanked him for his advice and for making time to meet with me.

After I left Elder Martinborough's office, I reflected on our conversation. No doubt, there were challenges ahead. Nonetheless, I resolved to trust God and continue in my pursuit to attend Caribbean Union College, God willing.

Chapter 12

Serving the Lord in the Classroom

As I worked to secure funding to attend Caribbean Union College, I continued teaching for the Ministry of Education. Much success attended my work with many of my students achieving high marks on their examinations and either entering the working world or continuing on with their schooling at a higher level. The parents in the community were very satisfied with the work I was doing with and for their children. On many occasions people remarked that I had a knack for teaching.

Many individuals, including prominent Ministry of Education officials, encouraged me to enter the local teachers' training college and pursue additional education in teaching. However, for a number of years, I kept putting off this form of training since I had my eyes set on attending CUC.

As it turned out, my attempts at securing funding to attend CUC proved a challenge. Therefore, while I waited on the Lord to come through for me in that regard, I thought seriously about what I could do in the meantime. It was at that time that I began to give serious thought to attending the local teachers' training college. I prayed and asked for God's leading and sought the advice of significant others.

From all indications, this was a worthwhile undertaking, so I decided to give it a shot. As a matter of fact, when I began to think seriously about entering the local Teacher's Training College, a close friend of mine remarked, "You had better do something constructive with your life in the meantime while you wait on the Lord to provide you with the financial means to attend CUC."

I had a special liking for mathematics and science. Therefore, my desire was to undergo a training program that would emphasize these two disciplines.

In 1982, I was offered a golden opportunity to do so. That year, in an attempt to fill the need for qualified mathematics and science teachers in the nation's schools, the Ministry of Education organized a specialist science and mathematics teacher training program for primary and secondary school teachers. I saw that as my chance to pursue formal teacher training.

Serving the Lord in the Classroom

It is interesting to note that I did not apply for admission into the program. On the contrary, it was the Ministry of Education who made me an offer. Taking into consideration my interest in the field of mathematics and science, my efforts to improve my teaching skills, and my potential usefulness in the teaching profession, the Ministry of Education wrote and invited me to attend an interview for possible acceptance into the program. Because of the distance between Georgetown and Long Creek, which was some thirty-four miles away, by the time the letter arrived the date for the interview had already passed. Notwithstanding this apparent setback, I presented myself for an interview at the Ministry of Education the day after I received the correspondence.

I explained to the officer that I had received the notice for the interview only the day before and, therefore, had come immediately. The interviewing officer accommodated my request and proceeded with the interview. I opted for the secondary track with a major in mathematics and a minor in science.

About two weeks into the 1982-83 academic year, I received written confirmation from the Ministry of Education that I was accepted into the three-year science/mathematics training program at the Lilian Dewar College of Education for Secondary Teachers.

One of the unique aspects of this special training program was its flexibility. I attended classes all day twice a week, and worked at my teaching job at Long Creek for the remaining three days of the school week. Consequently, I had ample time and scope to readily apply what I was being taught at college.

I enjoyed college life a lot. Each week I eagerly looked forward to attending classes. The study environment; the novelty of pursuing specialized training in mathematics and science, particularly chemistry; the expansion of my knowledge base both in the arts and sciences; the meaningful social interactions with faculty and students; the weekly assembly; the sporting activities; participation in student government; the enrichment activities; and the many opportunities for holistic development made college life a worthwhile experience. Additionally, the program engendered the respect of a large cross-section of society, and I felt honored to be involved in this special training program. Having to travel a far distance to and from college did not bother me one bit. The investment was more than worth the sacrifice involved.

During the last term of the first year, the college moved into a new building on the Cyril Potter College of Education compound at Turkeyen.

Toward the end of the first year of study, I faced a major challenge. All examinations were originally scheduled from Monday to Friday. I was scheduled to take my mathematics examinations on the first Friday of the examination week. However, one of our national holidays happened to fall on that particular

Thy Will Be Done

Friday. Consequently, the lecturer decided to conduct the examinations the next day, Saturday.

As a Seventh-day Adventist, this posed a special challenge for me. On Saturdays, as Jesus did, I attend church services and abstain from secular work and other personal pursuits. The day is essentially spent in worship of the Creator God and fostering Christian fellowship with other believers. To write the examinations on Saturday would have violated my conscience, so I resolved not to take the tests on that day.

I pleaded with the lecturer to change the examination date to one of the regular school days, but she did not grant to my request. I, therefore, took my case to the principal who decided to meet with me. As I walked into his office, the following dialog ensued.

"Alexander, how can I help you?"

"Well, sir, I have a major problem that needs your intervention." He leaned forward and surveyed me closely as I continued. "On account of the national holiday that falls on Friday, one of my examinations has been rescheduled for the next day, Saturday." He sat up in his chair as I continued. "As a Seventh-day Adventist, I worship God on Saturday. I, therefore, abstain from all worldly activities, including the study of secular subjects, and devote the twenty-four hours on that day to the worship of God. Consequently, I cannot write the examination on Saturday. I am, therefore, asking that the examination be rescheduled to another day."

"Alexander, I understand your religious convictions. But since this is only a one-time act in asking you to sit for your examination on a Saturday, I think that you should go ahead and take your examination on Saturday."

"Sir, if I do that I will be violating my conscience."

"Can't you ask your priest for a dispensation for one day so that you can write the examinations?"

"This is not a matter for the priest to decide. I am the one who must make a decision in this regard, and my conscience will not allow me to write the exams on Saturday."

"Have you spoken with the lecturer about this?"

"Yes, sir."

"And what did she say?"

"In spite of my plea to her to change the examination to another day, she insists that I write the examinations on Saturday."

"Well, as it stands, there is nothing I can do. I believe you will have to write the examinations on Saturday."

I left the principal's office that day feeling rather dejected. Nonetheless, I

Serving the Lord in the Classroom

purposed in my heart not to take the examination, whatever the consequence. I approached the president of the Guyana Conference of Seventh-day Adventists and asked for his advice. He challenged me to stand up for what I knew to be right, indicating that this was a test of my faith in God. He wrote a letter on my behalf asking that consideration be given to me to take my examination on another day.

I presented the letter to the relevant college officials, but there was no bending on their part. Notwithstanding my plea, the college went ahead and conducted the examination on Saturday. I did not show up for the exam, which made the lecturer very upset. My friends told me that in my absence she breathed out threats about what would happen to me as a consequence of not showing up for the exam.

I must admit that I had some foreboding about what might happen because of my non-compliance with the college's wishes. Nonetheless, I claimed the Bible promise that we must obey God rather than man. I, therefore, trusted God for His deliverance from the situation.

When I arrived on campus the following Monday, my friends greeted me, "Alexander, why you did not show up for the exam on Saturday? The lecturer is really upset with you. She wants to see you. You had better prepare yourself for a strong scolding from her in class this morning."

When the teacher entered the classroom that morning, I approached her before she had a chance to upbraid me in front of the other students.

"Miss, I learned that you wanted to see me."

She began, "So, Alexander, you did not show up for my exam on Saturday?"

"Miss, I explained to you why I could not write the examination on Saturday."

She vented her feelings and told me in no uncertain terms that she would not be scheduling another exam for those who deliberately opted not to show up on Saturday.

If the lecturer followed through with such a decision, my study program could be jeopardized because a student couldn't begin the second year of study until he would have passed all the first year courses. Therefore, unless something was done about the situation, I would not be able to continue with my study program at the college.

I hoped that the matter would be addressed before we were dismissed for the summer break; however, July came and the matter had not been resolved. I, therefore, spent a significant portion of the summer months worrying over the situation. As I examined my options, I knew that I was in for a tough time in trying to resolve this problem.

Thy Will Be Done

For one thing, the principal had already taken a stand on the matter, so approaching him again did not look like it would yield any positive results. The deputy principal was known to be rather intolerant of students with a religious persuasion like mine, so I did not believe that she would be inclined to make any representation on my behalf. I took the matter to God in prayer and pleaded with Him to intervene in His own way.

As it turned out, a series of events took place at the college during the summer months and leading into the first week of the new school year that served as my answer to prayer. About halfway through the summer vacation, the principal accepted a job offer in Australia and left. Consequently, the deputy principal was asked to act as principal in the interim. As the end of summer approached, a situation developed between the deputy principal and the Ministry of Education that resulted in her being asked to relinquish her position at the college. Therefore, by the start of the new school year, both the principal and deputy principal were no longer employed by the college. Thus God, through His providence, had begun to clear the way for me to be able to take my outstanding examination and, thereby, continue on with my study program.

With the departure of the deputy principal, the senior tutor was asked to assume leadership of the institution. This individual was known to be more understanding of my religious persuasion and was more amenable to settling the problem in a more amicable manner.

On the first day of the school term, I showed up for classes by faith. Upon arriving on campus, the acting principal called me into his office.

"Good morning, Alexander."

"Good morning, Sir."

"I have called you in connection with your study program. As I was browsing through your file, I discovered that you have not completed all your year one examinations…. Why is this so?"

"Sir, this has to do in part, with a stance I took based on my religious convictions. Two of my examinations that were originally scheduled for a Friday were rescheduled for Saturday because of the observance of one of our national religious festivals. As a Seventh-day Adventist, I do not engage in any secular activities, including the study of secular subjects, on Saturday. Rather, my Saturdays are devoted to religious worship to God, the creator of the universe. Therefore, I did not show up for the two examinations that were rescheduled for Saturday."

"Did you inform the college administration about your peculiar circumstances and seek to work out some alternative arrangement to take your examinations at a subsequent date?"

"Yes, sir. I did speak with the principal and the lecturer, but they did not come around to arranging for me to take the examinations on another date."

"Okay, Alexander, I will talk to the teachers concerned and have them prepare supplementary examinations. In the meantime, I will allow you to attend second year classes until such time as you write and pass the outstanding examinations for the first year."

"Thank you, sir, I am truly grateful for this gesture. I will be guided accordingly."

"You are most welcome, Alexander."

As I left the acting principal's office, I was overjoyed at the way God had worked through him to bring about a solution to the problem. I thanked God again and again for this. The onus was now on me to prepare for the examinations and give it my best shot.

I learned through one of my close friends that the lecturer was upset at having been told to prepare supplementary examinations. She hinted to some of my classmates that she would comply with the request of the acting principal but that she would make the exam very difficult. On learning about this, I alerted another Seventh-day Adventist student who had not taken the examination on Saturday either. We decided to study hard, pray for mercy on the part of the lecturer, and ask God for special intervention in the situation.

Within a few weeks of my meeting with the acting principal, we received confirmation about the new examination dates. And this time around, God be praised, no Saturdays were involved.

During the days leading up to the examinations, I immersed myself in study, asking God to guide me so that I could prepare as thoroughly as possible for the exams. At regular intervals during my preparation, I engaged in prayer and fasting.

On the evening before the mathematics examinations, I decided to visit the National Library in Georgetown and use the resources in the reference department to get some practice at answering mathematics questions that would likely be on the examinations. That evening I practiced answering questions until the library closed. Then I decided to fast and pray on the day of the examinations.

The following morning when I walked into the exam room I felt confident that in spite of how difficult the exam was, God would see me through. I prayed before I commenced work. Then I applied myself to the matter at hand.

I finished the science examinations and got ready for the mathematics examination in the afternoon. This was the subject area that I had the most foreboding about.

Thy Will Be Done

As an examination strategy, I went through the questions first and determined my approach before beginning to answer the questions. As I did so in this instance, something crossed my eyes. Right there before me were three or four identical questions to the ones which I had studied in the library the previous evening. Indeed, God was at work. I, therefore, included those questions among the ones I decided to attempt during the examinations.

I completed the exams during the time allotted. As I exited the room, I thanked God for His guidance throughout, and I left the results in His hands.

One Monday morning a few weeks later, I was coming out of the library when I saw the mathematics lecturer approaching at a brisk pace. She seemed to be in a good mood, so I began, "Good morning, miss!"

She slowed her pace. "Good morning, Alexander!" Somehow sensing that I had a query, she continued, "What's on your mind?"

"Miss, I would like to know if the results of my examinations are ready."

"Alexander, how do you think you did on the examinations?"

This was an unexpected question, and so as not to appear over confident, I retorted, "Miss, to be honest with you, I do not know."

Speaking in a serious tone, she said, "It is strange that you do not know how you did. *You* ought to at least have an idea as to how you performed on the examinations, Alexander!"

This encounter was not turning out to be what I had anticipated. As she uttered her last words, she increased her pace again and moved on. When she was almost out of earshot she called back to me, "You can check with the acting principal about the examination results."

By the time she had finished uttering those words, she was out of sight.

Not wanting to prolong the drama any longer, I headed straight for the acting principal's office. I met him along the way. Before I could ask him about the results, he said, "Alexander, I have been looking for you all morning. Where were you?"

"I was in the library for the most part of the morning after which I had a brief conversation with my mathematics lecturer."

"Well, Alexander, you can go and celebrate with the boys because you have passed your examinations."

"Thank you, sir, for sharing this good news with me! I also want to thank you for being instrumental in putting things in place to have me write the exams."

"You are most welcome, Alexander."

I felt as though a burden had rolled off my shoulders. Later on during the day when I saw my friend who had faced the same challenge as I did, she informed me that the acting principal had also told her that she had passed. We thanked God for working things out for us. At the first opportunity, I went to the mathematics lecturer and thanked her for allowing me to take my exams after all.

This experience strengthened my faith and confidence in God.

Overall, I found the remainder of my college life exciting and enjoyable. Before I knew it, I was down to my end of final year examinations. By God's grace and much hard work, I successfully completed the science/mathematics teacher training program. Thus, in June of 1986, I graduated from college as a trained Grade I Class I Teacher. This was a signal achievement in my life that would pave the way for the accomplishment of greater things.

Chapter 13

Where to Now?

After completion of the teacher training program, I remained in active employment at the Long Creek Government School. As I applied my newly acquired knowledge, I found myself enjoying my job more than ever. My services were much sought after in several schools across the nation.

Sometimes while traveling by bus to and from the city or when I met former classmates from college, they commended me for doing an outstanding job as a teacher. Some individuals even told me that many felt that I was a truly gifted teacher.

From all appearances, in the eyes of many, teaching as a vocation held good promise for me. I became so engrossed with teaching that I began to entertain thoughts of further study of mathematics so that I could teach at the college level. I even entertained thoughts of pursuing a doctor of arts (DA) degree in teaching with a major in mathematics. I actually located an institution in the United States that offered such a program. As I surveyed the content of the program, I felt that that was the ideal program I would like to pursue.

However, even as I sought to pursue further study in the line of teaching, I still found myself preoccupied with attending Caribbean Union College to train as a pastor.

In addition to pursuing further training in teaching or entering Caribbean Union College to study for the ministry, there was another option of pursuing an undergraduate degree in mathematics either full time or part time at the University of Guyana. Then there was the option of continuing in my current job as a teacher in the government system.

I was at a crossroads in regard to my choice of a future career. The critical question was, "What course of action should I take?"

Taking the admonition from Scripture that, "Whatsoever thy hands findeth to do, do it with thy might" (Eccl. 9:10), I decided to continue teaching and look for God's leading along the way.

Two years after completing teacher training college I was still working for the Ministry of Education. During that period I gave myself to much prayer and fasting about my career choice from the options at my disposal.

Where to Now?

I felt like the prophet Jeremiah who, speaking of his call to ministry exclaimed, "Thy words were found, and I did eat them; and thy word was unto me the joy and rejoicing of mine heart" (Jer. 15:16). I felt a compelling desire and a sustained urge to enter the ministry. It was as though I could not do without being involved in ministry as my major life vocation.

With such a compulsion, I again began to give serious thought about entering CUC and studying for the ministry. Thus, in November 1986, I applied for a tuition scholarship from the Guyana Conference of Seventh-day Adventist to study at CUC during the 1987-88 academic year.

While still teaching, I applied for admission into the theology program at CUC. In the event that I did not succeed in securing funding to start my studies at Caribbean Union College, I also applied for admission into the University of Guyana simultaneously to pursue a degree in mathematics and physics that same year.

I subsequently gained acceptance into Caribbean Union College and the University of Guyana simultaneously.

I felt excited about being accepted into CUC. The novelty of the prospect of actually pursuing theological training really inspired me. However, even as I cherished the thought of this impending reality, I was mindful of the fact that finances could prove to be the critical factor as to whether or not I started the program that year.

As I read through the financial information section of the CUC bulletin, I began to experience some serious misgivings. The actual cost of tuition, room, and board at CUC for the 1987-88 academic year was approximately $34,000 in local currency. When this figure was multiplied by four, I got the mammoth sum of $136,000. With the exchange rate for the United States dollar being G$4.25 to US$1.00, this amounted to US$32,000 for my complete study program.

From the depths of my heart, I knew that acquiring the sum necessary for my first year would prove to be a major challenge, much less the cost for four years. The following entry dated April 22, 1987, was made in my diary: "At present, I do not possess *any* money with which to defray college expenses. I am hoping and trusting, by faith, that the Lord will help me to secure a tuition scholarship from the Guyana Conference of Seventh-day Adventists. I will continually plead to God for His providence herein."

Despite the financial constraints I faced, in my eagerness to enter CUC, I devised a financial plan by which I hoped to secure enough funds to be able to attend.

As it turned out, for some reason unknown to me, my application for a tuition scholarship from the Guyana Conference of Seventh-day Adventists was

Thy Will Be Done

not approved. When I spoke to Pastor Lawrence London, the education director of the conference, he informed me that the conference was probably not going to offer any new scholarships that year but rather would likely consider applicants who were already at CUC and were struggling to finish off their studies. He said that my request would be discussed sometime in the future.

The financial plan I had designed proved futile. It soon became clear to me that my wish to attend CUC for the 1987-88 academic year was not going to come through.

This being the case, I decided to pursue my alternative plan. I, therefore enrolled in the mathematics/physics program at the University of Guyana for the 1987-88 school year as a part-time student. I felt confident that this was the way the Lord was leading at this point of my life, and I resolved to follow through with it.

Even as I started my studies at the university, I determined to continue seeking out sources of funding to study at CUC.

I asked the Lord to continue unfolding His plans for my future, and I prayed earnestly that He would grant me success in my academic pursuits at the University of Guyana.

Chapter 14

God's Providence

Combining university work and study with traveling long distances to and from classes proved to be very challenging. I had secured release and permission from the Ministry of Education to leave school at 2:00 p.m. each day to travel to classes some forty miles away. But by the time I returned home each night, it was around 9:00 p.m. To make matters worse, public transportation proved rather unreliable at times, causing me to have to wait for long hours on the road to and from classes. On some occasions I missed classes because of the long wait and the lateness of the arrival of transportation. In spite of the challenges, I survived my first year of study at the university.

Depending on how the Lord led, if I continued my study program at the university the following school year, I knew I would have to give serious thought to studying full time for the remainder of my program there. Since that would mean resigning from my teaching job, I would have to secure sponsorship to be able to do so.

Based on my earlier conversation with Pastor London, I was hopeful that something should have been in the pipeline as regards to the award of a tuition scholarship from the Guyana Conference for the 1988-89 school year. However, by June 1988, I had not gotten any further feedback from the conference regarding the tuition scholarship award. This was cause for concern. The future seemed quite uncertain. From all appearances, my entrance into Caribbean Union College for the 1988-89 school year was in jeopardy.

While this was taking place, I continued to have dreams in which I was actively carrying on the work of God. Even though circumstances seemed foreboding, I took this as a sign that God wanted me to keep my hopes alive as far as entering the ministry was concerned.

One day in late June of that same year, I dropped by the conference office to pick up some quarterlies. As I was making my way out of the Adventist Book Center, I saw Pastor London coming down the stairs. When he saw me he called out, "Alexander, what are your plans right now as far as studying is concerned?"

"Well, pastor, I am currently enrolled at the University of Guyana."

Thy Will Be Done

"That's good. Do you still plan on attending CUC?"

"Yes, pastor, but as you know, I am financially strapped."

"The conference may be in a position to offer you a tuition scholarship to study at CUC for the 1988-89 academic year. However, even if you receive the scholarship, it will not be enough. You will need to get additional funds to be able to meet educational costs at CUC not covered by the scholarship award. What have you been doing by way of fundraising to attend CUC?"

"Pastor, to be honest with you, there is not much I can do in this regard. I have attempted to save a portion of my salary, but because of economic constraints, this has met with very little success. Other attempts at raising money for school have also failed."

"Do your best to raise some funds for college."

"By faith, I certainly will, pastor"

After speaking with Pastor London, I felt somewhat encouraged. I thanked the Lord for His leading thus far and asked that His will be done.

I later learned that earlier in the year Pastor Roy McGarrell had written the education director of the conference recommending me for consideration for a tuition scholarship. In his letter he mentioned that I had been awarded a tuition scholarship from the conference during his term as president but that I had been unable to utilize the scholarship offer at that time.

I decided to pray and fast on June 22 in hopes of determining the Lord's will in the matter. During my conversations with the Lord that day, I asked that His will would be done in my life with regards to my desire to enter Caribbean Union College. I prayed earnestly that His blessings would continue to rest upon me as He led me into a deeper and more meaningful relationship with Him each day. I prayed for grace to be able to continually submit my will to His will for the rest of my life.

I prayed further that I would so train myself not merely to obey Him but to agree with His decisions and follow them, not because I had to, but because my soul willed it. I submitted my freedom of choice to God. If He willed something for me, I willed it too. If He did not will it, I did not wish it. In all life's situations, my prayer was that I be granted the spirit of discernment to be sure of the wise and loving will of God no matter what I felt. By so doing I felt confident in facing life's challenges, conquering them, and defeating them by the power of God at work in my life.

My prayers also ascended to God on behalf of the Silver Hill SDA church building program. I sought the Lord's help as I did my best in setting the building machinery in place so that if I should have to leave for Caribbean Union College before its completion that the work would continue without interruption.

God's Providence

Later that day I dispatched a letter to Pastor Roy McGarrell in the United States requesting some financial assistance to defray the cost of my first year's study at CUC. I also wrote CUC and indicated that I was planning on enrolling for the 1988-89 academic year and that I would, therefore, like to have an official letter from the college indicating that I was accepted as a student for the 1988-89 academic year.

It was the middle of July, and no firm word had been received from Pastor London regarding the tuition scholarship to study at CUC. So as not to end up in a similar situation as the previous year, I began to explore avenues for the funding needed to continue my study program at the University of Guyana on a full-time basis. Apart from the ease of time management that studying on a full-time basis would afford, information from the University of Guyana was indicating that they would not be offering the part-time degree program in mathematics from the 1988-89 academic year.

In my quest for sponsorship to study at the University of Guyana, I came across an offer from the Inter-American Development Bank (IDB) that held good prospects. The bank was offering grants to finance full-time study at the University of Guyana for the 1988-89 school year, so I decided to apply for a grant from that financial institution.

As I prepared to file the application to the IDB, I was aware of the dilemma I would face if offered funding from this organization and the Guyana Conference of Seventh-day Adventists at the same time. If that happened, I would have to choose between the two offers. Alternatively, if plans fell through in regards to being able to attend CUC, my back-up plan would be to pursue the offer from the IDB to continue my studies at the University of Guyana.

On the other hand, my resolve was that if I was granted a scholarship from the Guyana Conference, I would abandon the mathematics program and proceed to CUC forthwith.

As July came to an end, I still had not received any definite communication from Pastor London on the tuition scholarship to study at CUC. In order to meet the deadline for the submission of applications for the grant from the IDB to study at the University of Guyana on a full-time basis, I went ahead and submitted an application.

As the start of the 1988-89 academic year loomed ahead, I returned to the drawing board regarding my career choice. To that end, I declared August 15 a day of prayer and fasting. During the day, I reiterated to God my strong conviction that I was being called to enter the ministry. I told the Lord that the road ahead seemed uncertain in regards to when I would actually embark

Thy Will Be Done

on my theological training at CUC. I also mentioned the fact that other career opportunities, including further studies at the University of Guyana, were beckoning me. I recapped with the Lord that it had been some time since I had first applied for financial assistance from the Guyana Conference of Seventh-day Adventists to study at CUC. I entreated Him to open this door of financial assistance or some other means according to His will for my life.

Notwithstanding my earnest entreaties, I asked Him to help me decide on the best course of action should His providence dictate that I remain in Guyana a little longer. If I did, I would have to choose between continuing teaching or embarking on full-time study at the University of Guyana.

As a sign, I asked the Lord to open the door He wanted me to go through. Whichever of the two organizations—the Guyana Conference of Seventh-day Adventists or the IDB—sent me a confirmation letter for a scholarship award first, I would take that to be God's will for my life. Furthermore, I told the Lord that if confirmation of the award of a scholarship from the Guyana Conference of Seventh-day Adventists came first, I would also take that as a sign of my call to the ministry.

Two days later, I received a package from CUC in the mail. The college needed some additional information to be able to update my file in preparation for the 1988-89 academic year. Before mailing the requested information, I decided to contact the secretary of the Guyana Conference of Seventh-day Adventists for an update on my scholarship request. If the conference had awarded me a tuition scholarship to enter CUC that same year, I would go ahead and mail the information back to the college. If not, I would hold off on returning the forms to CUC.

I called the conference office and asked to speak with Pastor London for an update on my application. However, I was told that he was out of the country at that time. I was, therefore, informed that I needed to speak with Brother Clement Tiexeira, the conference treasurer. He was also a member of the Scholarship and Education Committees.

I was transferred to Brother Tiexeira's office. "Good morning, Brother Tiexeira. This is Brother Alexander Isaacs, elder of the Silver Hill SDA Church."

"Hello, Brother Isaacs, how can I help you this morning?"

"I am calling in connection with my application for a tuition scholarship from the Guyana Conference of Seventh-day Adventists to study at CUC for the 1988-89 academic year. The start of school is a few weeks away, and I have not yet received any official word from the conference as to whether I will receive the scholarship for the upcoming academic year. Could you please let me know if this matter has already been addressed by the Education Committee and what has been the outcome?"

He waited a few seconds as if trying to absorb the mouthful of information I had thrown at him. "Brother Isaacs, I am glad you called because a few days ago the Education Committee met to review applications and award tuition scholarships to CUC for the 1988-89 academic year. Your application was considered along with the others. The committee has reached a decision in your favor, and you will be awarded a two-year tuition scholarship to study at Caribbean Union College."

Those words were like apples of gold in pictures of silver. As they fell on my ear, gratitude for God's magnanimous workings on my behalf welled up in my heart. "Praise God! And thank you for sharing this bit of information with me! I am overjoyed."

"You are most welcome, Brother Isaacs. I guess you will be hearing officially from the Education Committee on this soon."

"So what should I do in the meantime?"

"Well, even though the award has been voted, I must let you know that there is a precondition to the award."

"What is the precondition that the committee has stipulated?"

I waited for his response with a measure of trepidation. "This is it. Your tuition scholarship award was granted with the precondition that you first gain acceptance into CUC for the 1988-89 academic year. Have you been accepted into CUC for the ensuing school year?"

"Well, I gained acceptance into CUC for the 1987-88 school year. However, I could not attend then due to financial constraints. I contacted the college earlier this year and informed them that I was desirous of starting my study program there from the 1988-89 academic year. A couple of days ago, I received a package from CUC requesting various bits of information in order to finalize my acceptance into CUC for the 1988-1989 academic year. It was as a result of my receipt of that package from the college that I decided to call the conference for an update on my scholarship request before returning the requested information to CUC."

"Excellent! Now, since this is the case, why not come in to the conference office in order to get further details on the scholarship award?"

"Most surely! I will come in today."

I was excited at receiving this news. When I got off the telephone, I thanked the Lord for the outworking of His will in my life at this critical juncture. This kind of news was many years in coming, but it had indeed come when I needed it most.

I hurried over to my stepmother's place of work and shared the good news with her. She was happy to learn that I had succeeded in securing the

Thy Will Be Done

scholarship. As we conversed further on the matter, I voiced some concerns regarding a few items of business that would have to be taken care of while I would be away from Guyana. Foremost among them was the payment of my insurance premiums. After a brief moment of silence, she said, "Alex, don't worry about that. I will make the monthly payments for you while you are at school." I gave her a big hug and thanked her for her generosity. Then she said, "Son, you had better travel to Georgetown without any further delay to get more details about the scholarship offer from the conference." Within the space of half an hour, I left for Georgetown by bus.

Upon arrival at the conference office, I met with Pastor London's secretary, Debbie Gittens. Debbie and I exchanged some pleasantries before I sought to clarify some issues pertaining to my tuition scholarship award. She then asked that I contact the associate education director, Margaret Ramsarran, for further details. Margaret sought to ascertain my interest in attending CUC and offered some advice regarding my imminent departure to college.

That afternoon I mailed the information that CUC had requested.

On my way home, I reflected on the events of the day. God's providential workings were made manifest in ways unimaginable. In one day I had gotten answers to important questions that had been unanswered for several years. The way was now clear for me to enter CUC. But most importantly, the die had been cast—the award of the tuition scholarship confirmed my call to the ministry, the "call" I had been wrestling with and waiting on for many years. It had finally come in an unmistakable sign, and I thanked God for the revelation of His will for my life.

I had a mere three weeks in which to make ready for my departure to CUC. Nonetheless, I was prepared to give it my best shot.

When I arrived home that afternoon, I briefed my family on my trip to the conference office. Later that evening, I wrote in my diary:

"This is nothing short of the hand of God at work in my affairs. God be thanked again and again for His wonderful love and revelation of His plan for my life. I am determined to follow wherever He leads with the assurance that wherever His plans lead me He makes Himself responsible for my success. I am resolved to do nothing that is outside His will for my life. Ride on King Jesus!"

Chapter 15

CUC at Last

The day after my meeting with officials at the Guyana Conference of Seventh-day Adventists office, I turned in my resignation from my teaching job with the Ministry of Education.

When I went to church that weekend at Silver Hill, my sermon was titled "He is Able." This was part of my public thanksgiving to God. I recounted some of the blessings He had strewn along my pathway ever since I had surrendered my life to Him. I reminded the brethren that God is able to do exceeding abundantly above all that we my think, ask, or desire.

On Sunday during my morning devotions, I poured out my heart to God about the formidable challenge of coming up with the supplementary finances required to travel to CUC. I made the following entry in my diary:

"Our heavenly Father, I bow my knees unto You in adoration. I approach Your throne of grace with the confidence that You exist and that You reward those who diligently seek You.

"Lord, as revealed through Your providential workings, You have called me to the gospel ministry. The award of a tuition scholarship from the Guyana Conference of Seventh-day Adventists has confirmed Your desire for me to enter the sacred ministry and attend Caribbean Union College. This is seen as the 'green light' for me, and I wish to follow Your lead.

"Father, this call has come at a time when I am in dire financial need. As it stands now, I need an absolute minimum of G$8,475 to take care of expenses associated with my planned entrance into CUC for the 1988-89 academic year, outside of the funding to be received through the tuition scholarship award. I do not have this amount. When I subtract what I currently have in cash, the remainder needed is approximately $8,000.

"Lord, like the prophet Hezekiah of old, I take this opportunity to spread my need out before You because the situation is beyond my capacity to handle, and only Your divine intervention will suffice. Father in heaven, I am depending on you to advise me on what to do. May Your leading hand be ever before me as I follow Your direction and may Your Holy Spirit implant right convictions all the way through.

Thy Will Be Done

"Lord, as it stands now, the only airline that has a vacant seat for me to be able to travel to Trinidad in time for the beginning of classes in September is BWIA. By faith I have gone ahead and reserved a seat on that airline. However, the ticket has to be paid for in US currency. Please lead me to a source of funding to meet this need.

"Please hear my prayer, O God, and grant me Your peace. With thanks in advance for hearing and answering my prayer through Jesus Christ my Lord, amen."

After laying out my case to the Lord, I was impressed to approach a number of individuals who had been encouraging me all along to attend CUC. As a start, my father and stepmother donated G$1,000 each. Then one of my cousins pledged G$500. In addition, my eldest sister and husband loaned me some money. The Emmanuel Seventh-day Church pledged another G$1,000, and on and on it went. In short, within one week of confirmation of my receipt of the tuition scholarship, I was able to raise approximately G$7,000 (approximately US$1,650). This was a good exercise in faith, and I viewed it as God's endorsement of my plan to study at Caribbean Union College.

I then contacted Pastor and Sister Roy McGarrell in the United States of America and asked them to assist me with the US currency to purchase my airline ticket to Trinidad. God be praised that in spite of other pressing family commitments that they had at that time, the McGarrells were inclined to help. I believed, by faith, that my request to them would be granted.

A few days later when I contacted the McGarrells for an update on my request, to my delight, they told me that they would purchase my airline ticket to Trinidad. Actually, they had already authorized the dispatch of my ticket through a BWIA airline agent in Michigan. I was further told that when I was ready to leave for Trinidad all I needed to do was go in to the BWIA office in Georgetown and pick up my ticket. I thanked them for such a timely gesture and I thanked God for rewarding my faith once more.

The rapidity with which things were moving toward my actual departure for Caribbean Union College was almost unbelievable. It was evident that God was at the helm of my affairs. This further strengthened my belief that this was His will for my life at this juncture. He is indeed a living God, a Father to me, and a giver of gifts to those who diligently seek Him. I recommitted myself to staying within the orbit of His will for my life with the conviction that, as Ellen G. White states, "When we give ourselves wholly to God and in our work follow His directions, He makes Himself responsible for its accomplishment" (*Christ's Object Lessons,* p. 363). Praise God from whom all blessings flow.

CUC at Last

By September 7, five days before my departure to Trinidad, there were still several outstanding matters that needed to be attended to. I held a day of prayer and fasting on that same day to solicit the Lord's blessing on my entry into the ministry; His choice of a new leader to take over the leadership of the Silver Hill Seventh-day Adventist Church; success in the uplifting of my airline ticket for travel to Trinidad on September 11; and success in final negotiations pertaining to my acceptance into CUC for the upcoming academic year.

Up to that point I had not received final confirmation from CUC as to whether I had been accepted for the 1988-89 school year. At about mid-morning during the day of prayer and fasting, I contacted CUC by telephone and inquired about the status of my acceptance into the theology program. To my delight, I was told that I had been officially accepted for the 1988-89 academic year. The official in the Registrar's Office who disclosed this information to me asked whether I had already finalized travel arrangements. I answered in the affirmative and told her that my departure date was September 11 on BWIA at 9:15 p.m. She took my ticket reference number and said that the dean of students of the college would be at the Piarco International Airport to meet me upon my arrival in Trinidad. I thanked God for helping me clear that particular hurdle.

I traveled to Georgetown and contacted the BWIA office to see whether my ticket had arrived from the United States. On inquiry, I learned that the ticket had not yet arrived. However, my seat reservation was still in tact. The airline asked that I check back with the office later in the day. When I checked back, I was told that nothing had changed. Though somewhat daunted, I had a strong conviction that I would receive my airline ticket in due course.

Later that evening after I returned home, I traveled to Silver Hill for a farewell service that my church had planned for me.

Three days before my intended departure to CUC, my ticket had still not arrived. When I checked with the BWIA office in Georgetown, the ticket agent said that the airline had not received any word from their office in Michigan about my ticket.

Around 12:30 p.m. I went to the Guyana telephone and telegraph office and placed a call to Pastor McGarrell for an update.

"Good afternoon, Pastor McGarrell. This is Brother Isaacs calling from Guyana."

"Hello, Brother Isaacs. Did you get my message that I left for you at the conference office?"

"No, I did not receive any message from the conference office."

"Well, I called the conference office earlier in the week and asked that they

Thy Will Be Done

pass on a message to you to call me today at 12:30 p.m."

Taken aback by this revelation, I exclaimed, "Indeed!"

"Yes. As a matter of fact, Sister McGarrell and I were sitting right here by the telephone waiting for your call. So when you called, we thought you were doing so in response to the message I had left for you at the conference office."

"What a coincidence! I believe God, through His angels, led me to call you at this particular time."

"We concur with you on this, Brother Isaacs. God has indeed guided you to call us at this time."

"Well, Alexander, the reason we asked you to call was to update you on the matter of your airline ticket for travel to CUC. Did you receive the ticket from the BWIA Guyana office?

"No, Pastor McGarrell. I checked the BWIA office in Guyana twice this morning, and they said that no ticket is there for me."

"On Tuesday, September 6, when Sister McGarrell and I contacted the BWIA office in Berrien Springs, Michigan, they gave us permission to purchase a one-way ticket for you to travel to Trinidad, which we did. The airline assured us that everything was okay and that the ticket would be transmitted to the BWIA Guyana office for you to pick up. However, when I called the airline office later in the week, to my surprise and dismay, I was told that the airline had not consented to dispatch your ticket to Guyana. The reason they gave was that a non-resident of Trinidad and Tobago must have a return ticket for travel to that island. I explained to the airline agent that you had already been officially accepted into Caribbean Union College and would be embarking on a four-year study program there. Consequently, there wasn't anything clandestine about your intended trip to Trinidad."

"And what did they say in reply?"

"Even though I pleaded with them to allow you to travel on a one-way ticket, which was already purchased on your behalf, they were unrelenting in their stance on the matter."

As Pastor McGarrell spoke, I began to feel uneasy. He continued. "I appealed to the manager at the Michigan office to allow you to travel to Trinidad on a one-way ticket. After a lot of back and forth dialog on the subject, he finally came around to saying that the stance that his office had taken was in accordance with the wishes of the Guyana and Trinidad governments."

"I am very appreciative of all the efforts put forward by you to seek the release of my ticket to travel to Trinidad. What else can be done in the situation?"

"Alexander, we have got to continue praying that God will work something out in your favor. In the meantime, I would suggest that you contact the

BWIA Georgetown office in Guyana and ask them to contact the BWIA office in Michigan and request that your ticket be released."

"Thank you, pastor, I will contact the BWIA Guyana office as soon as I get off the telephone."

By the time I was through talking with Pastor McGarrell and rushed to the BWIA Georgetown office, it had already closed for the day. The guard informed me that it was not possible for me to speak with any of the airline officials until the following day. Other efforts to contact the office later that day proved futile.

I tried two other airlines to see if I could get a seat out of Guyana on Sunday, September 11, but no vacant seats were available. I was therefore stuck with BWIA if I were to get to Trinidad in time for registration on September 12.

I could not do anything further about the matter until the following day when I planned to consult with the BWIA officials in Georgetown. It was clear that this matter needed divine intervention. I spread out my case before God through prayer and claimed the victory. I reminded the Lord of the issues involved and asked Him to put words of wisdom in my mouth as to what to say when I spoke with the airline officials the next day about the release of my ticket. I asked Him to work things out to my advantage. I begged Him to send His angels before me to prepare the way for victory and that He Himself should superintend my progress. I also enlisted the support of the membership of the Silver Hill SDA Church by way of special prayers to God that the matter be solved so that I could be issued with my ticket for travel to Trinidad.

The following morning I was the first person to arrive at the airline office in Georgetown. That particular morning the office opened later than normal. Notwithstanding, I was the first customer to be attended to.

As I approached the ticketing counter, I felt impressed to use a direct approach to ascertaining whether my ticket had arrived. Fortunately for me as I approached the counter I realized that the individual who would be helping me was the same person with whom I had spoken the previous day. Therefore, rather than starting our dialog with the circumstances surrounding the issuance of my ticket by the Michigan office, I got straight to the point.

"Good morning, madam. I am the individual who spoke with you yesterday about the arrival of my ticket from the United States for me to travel to Trinidad tomorrow. Can you tell me if the ticket has arrived?"

"What's your name again?"

"Alexander Isaacs."

"Let me check the system."

Thy Will Be Done

While she checked the system, I prayed that she would come back with a positive answer.

"Mr. Isaacs, your ticket has arrived!"

"Indeed!"

"Yes, it was sent yesterday afternoon."

Her words were like music to my ears. I instantly felt a great relief. As it turned out, after our telephone conversation on Friday, Pastor McGarrell, in his efforts to secure me a ticket to be able to travel to CUC, stumbled upon another travel agent a few buildings away from the one which had refused to issue me a one way ticket. As he recalled, when he asked to purchase a one way ticket for me to travel to Trinidad, he was pleasantly surprised when the travel agent granted the request without any preconditions. He was therefore able to purchase a one way ticket for me to travel to Trinidad after all. He had called the BWIA office in Michigan and succeeded in getting them to dispatch my ticket to the BWIA Guyana office.

Normally, the next step would be the issuance of my ticket by the clerk. However, that did not happen. After she pulled up my ticket details and was about to issue my ticket, she excused herself for a brief moment and went to speak with the manager. After several minutes, she returned to the counter and said, "Mr. Isaacs, the manager has indicated that there are some restrictions pertaining to the issuance of your ticket."

"Could you please tell me what those restrictions are?"

"The manager will speak to you further on this matter."

A few minutes later, I was ushered into the manager's office.

"Mr. Isaacs, your ticket was transmitted to our office yesterday afternoon. However, there are certain conditions that have to be met before this office can release your ticket."

I sat up in my chair and braced myself for what was to follow. "The airline has an agreement with the governments of Guyana and Trinidad and Tobago not to issue non-residents of Trinidad and Tobago with one-way tickets to travel into that twin-island republic. Since your ticket is a one-way ticket, this poses some difficulty as regards to your intended travel to Trinidad and Tobago."

"But now that the ticket is actually here and the purpose of my visit to Trinidad is to study, what are the options at my disposal as far as traveling to Trinidad on a one-way ticket is concerned?"

"I have spoken with our Michigan office, and they have authorized the release of your ticket on two conditions. First, you will have to produce an official letter of acceptance to CUC. The second condition is that you acquire some form of documentation from the Trinidad and Tobago Consul in Guyana

CUC at Last

granting a waiver of the regulations governing a non-Trinidad and Tobago national traveling to that state on a one-way ticket. Once you comply with these two conditions, you can collect your ticket for travel."

With a prayer in my heart, I hurried off to make contact with the Trinidad and Tobago Consul. Through God's providential workings, I was able to gain an audience with the Trinidad and Tobago high commissioner in Georgetown. I outlined to him my present circumstances and entreated his assistance in securing the release of my airline ticket.

The high commissioner requested a letter from the Guyana Conference of Seventh-day Adventists confirming that I had been accepted into Caribbean Union College for the 1988-89 academic year. He also needed proof from the Guyana Conference of Seventh-day Adventists that I had indeed been granted a tuition scholarship from that body to study at CUC. The high commissioner promised that once I provided those bits of information, he would grant a written waiver allowing me to enter Trinidad and Tobago on a one-way ticket as well as authorize the release of my ticket from the BWIA Guyana office.

In light of the prevailing circumstances, he advised that I push back my departure date to Trinidad by one day to Monday, September 12. I thanked him for his understanding and advice and pledged to present the necessary documents early on Monday.

I returned to the airline office and told them about the outcome of my meeting with the high commissioner. At the same time, I took the opportunity to request a change of flight date as suggested by the high commissioner. The counter clerk made the change. However, all the flights out to Trinidad on Monday were filled, so I was put on standby for the 9:15 p.m. flight on Monday night. I thanked the airline officials for their assistance and left.

I then made my way to church at Silver Hill where the brethren had been praying for my success in receiving my airline ticket and waiting for me to arrive to conduct a farewell communion service that was scheduled for that day. Upon arriving at church, the service was already underway. When I showed up, the membership breathed a sigh of relief and greeted me. "Did you get through?" they all asked in unison.

"I have gotten through to a certain extent, but I will not be able to pick up my ticket until Monday. My departure date has, therefore, been pushed back by one day." I then thanked the church members for their prayers on my behalf for God's special intervention. I joined in with the church service and led out in the communion service.

After the communion service was over, I participated in a sumptuous farewell lunch that the church had specially prepared for me.

Thy Will Be Done

That Sabbath afternoon I conducted a special Bible study at church and handled pertinent church-related matters. I also officially handed over the leadership of the Silver Hill Church to my successor. Before leaving church that afternoon, I charged the church leadership and members to be faithful unto the coming of the Lord and to continue working faithfully for the advancement of His kingdom.

When I returned to Long Creek that evening, I attended a farewell party at my parents' residence. Many friends and well-wishers were there, and they conveyed their best wishes for a safe journey and success in my educational pursuits. Being the first resident from my village to train as a teacher and now about to embark on ministerial training at CUC made the villagers proud.

On Sunday, September 11, I finalized travel arrangements for my trip to the airport the following day in preparation for my flight out of Guyana. I also did as much packing of my personal belongings and some needed items for college as I possibly could in anticipation of possible delays that may occur on the morrow as I sought to wrap up arrangements for my trip to Trinidad.

That night I hardly slept. I passed most of the time rather pensively. I had mixed thoughts and feelings about what the new day would bring forth as I finalized plans for travel to Trinidad. Beyond that, I found myself preoccupied with what the future might hold for me now that I would be leaving the shores of Guyana after all. I had longed for this opportunity, but now that it was about to become reality, I did not seem as anxious to leave as I was before. It was well after 2:00 a.m. when I finally dozed off to sleep.

When I awoke later that morning, it was almost dawn. In light of the important matters still to be cleared up in order for me to travel to Trinidad that night, I decided to pray and fast. I had a rather engaging and prolonged devotion that was interspersed with special petitions to God for His continued guidance in my life and especially the unfolding of the day's activities, particularly the release of my ticket from the airline office.

After my devotion I caught the first available means of transportation to the city, in this instance it involved hitching a ride on a cargo truck on its way to Georgetown from the hinterlands of Guyana. However, the truck did not go all the way into the city. At the point where I was dropped off, a distance of a little under a mile from the city, transportation into the city was slow in coming. Therefore, in the interest of time, I ended up having to beg a youngster for a ride into the city on his bicycle. The lad willingly consented, only that, in this case, I rode all the way into town while he sat on the tow bar of the bicycle.

When we finally rolled into town, I was covered with sweat. There was

CUC at Last

no time to lose. I headed straight to the Guyana Conference of Seventh-day Adventists headquarters. On arrival there, I asked to speak with the education director's secretary, Deborah Gittens. After laying out my peculiar circumstances to her, I asked her to prepare a letter addressed to the Trinidad and Tobago high commissioner authenticating my acceptance into CUC as well as my award of a scholarship from the conference. She willingly assisted me with my request. I sat in her office and waited anxiously for the letter. No doubt sensing the anxiety in my manner, she sought to calm me by saying, "Brother Isaacs, take it easy. Everything will work out just fine." With such reassurance, I bided my time. When the letter was eventually ready, I collected it, thanked her, and hurried off with it to the high commissioner's office.

Unfortunately, the high commissioner's office was not easily accessible by the use of public transportation. Therefore, again, in the interest of time, I had to hitch another ride on a bicycle in a similar manner to how I had traveled earlier that morning.

On arrival at the high commissioner's office, I learned that he was out on an errand and would be back at around 11:00 a.m. Rather than sit around and wait on his return, I informed his secretary that I would return in an hour's time, and I rushed off to attend to a few other pressing matters.

Providentially, while shopping in a popular department store in the city, I ran into the high commissioner. I told him that I had stopped by his office earlier to seek his assistance in releasing my airline ticket. After a brief exchange, he asked that I meet him in his office in fifteen minutes. I immediately left off shopping and made my way to his office. On arrival there, the secretary informed me that the high commissioner had arrived a couple of minutes ago. I was then ushered in to meet with him once more.

I handed over to him the documentation from the Guyana Conference. After reading through the letter, he proceeded to prepare the letter of waiver.

Within half an hour, the letter was ready. It was addressed to the immigration officer in charge at the Piarco International Airport with copies to the chief immigration officer at the Timehri International Airport and the BWIA office in Guyana. I thanked him and left for the BWIA ticket office.

On arrival at the ticket office, I presented my documents to the manager. Satisfied that I had complied with the requirements, he authorized the release of my ticket. Since I was on standby, he advised that I arrive at the airport at least one hour before the regular check-in time. I thanked the manager and left. My major hurdle was now crossed, and I glorified God for such an accomplishment. I thanked Him for intervening in my affairs once more and for clearing the way for me to be able to travel to Trinidad after all.

Thy Will Be Done

I completed my shopping, secured some foreign exchange from the Central Bank, and then began my homeward journey. Because of traffic congestion, my homeward journey was very slow. Upon arriving at home, everyone was anxious to hear how things went with regards to the release of my ticket. I proudly showed them my ticket, and everyone glorified God for His provision in such a marvelous way. I concurred with the hymn writer William Cowper who penned the words, "God moves in a mysterious way, His wonders to perform He plants His footsteps in the sea; And rides upon the storm."

After eating a light lunch, I finished packing, and with just under an hour to check in, I said goodbye to my parents, siblings, and friends. Parting was hard. Emotions ran high and many of us ended up in tears. Words of encouragement and advice assailed my ears: "Take good care of yourself." "We will really miss you." "We will pray for you." "Keep Guyana's flag flying high." "You must write and let us know how you are doing!"

Friends and relatives kept me company as I waited on the road for my transportation to the airport. Unfortunately, the vehicle from Linden that was to take me to the airport did not show up at the time agreed on. News subsequently got to us that the driver could not make it any longer.

At such late notice, it was difficult to make alternative arrangements that would guarantee my arrival at the airport on time. As precious time went ticking by, I began to feel uneasy. I paced up and down the road, worried about the fact that my check-in time was fast approaching and that I still had not yet departed for the airport.

Finally, in desperation, I began stopping every vehicle that came by in an attempt to hitch a ride to the airport. Just at about the time when the situation was getting too close for comfort, a pickup truck loaded with wood and charcoal stopped. After I explained my plight to the driver, he consented to give me a ride directly to the airport. The driver had to shift things around to create space to accommodate me in the vehicle. As a consequence, family members could not accompany me to the airport as was originally planned.

After I got into the vehicle, from my cramped position, I managed to wave goodbye to my friends and relatives. As the vehicle moved down the road, I could still see my folks waving as I looked into the rear view mirror. The vehicle then rounded a bend in the road and disappeared out of the sight of the small crowd which had gathered to see me off.

By the time we arrived at the airport, the airline had just begun to check in passengers. I thanked the driver for his kind assistance, disembarked and, headed straight for the check-in line. I experienced a certain degree of anxiety as I awaited my turn in the check in line. I kept a prayer in my heart that I would be fortunate enough to secure a seat on the flight.

To my delight, a little under an hour after check in had begun, I was called forward and allowed to check in on the flight. After I was through at the counter, I cleared immigration without any difficulty. Interestingly enough, the immigration officer did not even ask for the documentation I had received from the high commissioner earlier in the day. I joined the other passengers in the departure lounge awaiting the arrival of the aircraft, which was late. As soon as the incoming passengers had disembarked and the airplane had refueled, we were allowed to board.

This was my first trip by airplane, so I did not know what to expect. I was, therefore, somewhat uneasy. As I sat in my seat, I recounted the happenings in my life up to that point. As I did so, I could not help but conclude that God's guiding hands were at work all along. Now that I was actually leaving the shores of Guyana for CUC, I felt a sense of accomplishment. I could hardly believe that my quest to enter CUC was about to be realized.

I nervously sat in my seat and held my breath as the aircraft taxied up the runway and lifted into the air. I was actually on my way to Caribbean Union College, indeed! The unfamiliar sound of the wheels of the aircraft receding into their locked position caused goose pimples to surface on my skin. To my relief, the sound soon subsided, and I felt much more at ease.

As the airplane headed into the night sky, I felt mixed emotions. This was the first time I was leaving home for any extended period of time and traveling to a foreign country. What would life be like for me at Caribbean Union College? Would the high expectations I had of studying there be realized? How would I cope in a strange land? Would this be worth it after all? Time alone would tell.

Chapter 16

A New Beginning

I peered through the aircraft window into the night sky and saw the lights of the area surrounding the airport fading into the distance.

As I sat in my seat, I reflected on all that had led up to this moment. I felt satisfied at the way things had worked out after all. It was like a dream come through. I had no doubt in my mind whatsoever that this was part of God's purpose for my life.

The aircraft touched down in Trinidad about an hour and five minutes after departure. An official from the Dean of Students' Office at Caribbean Union College met me at the immigration desk. Again, I cleared immigration without any difficulty. As was the case in Guyana, the authorities did not ask for the documentation I had on me from the high commissioner. Before long, I collected my luggage, cleared customs, and boarded the vehicle that had been sent to take me to the college, which was about half an hour's drive from the airport.

By the time I arrived on campus, it was after 10:00 p.m. The residence hall assistant assigned me a temporary room to sleep in for the night with the assurance that I would be assigned my permanent room the following day. After placing my belongings in the assigned room, I surveyed the men's dormitory in an effort to become familiar with my new surroundings as best I could.

Before retiring to bed, I went to the water fountain on the ground floor at the southern end of the dormitory and took a long drink. Then I stood there and mused to myself about the goodness of God and the reality of being at CUC. I felt a sense of accomplishment at what God had done on my behalf. I then went back to my room, climbed into bed, and was soon sound asleep.

I was awakened the following morning to the sound of recorded music streaming from the dormitory rooms. Movements could be heard from various sections of the dormitory. I realized then that the male students were preparing for morning worship in the men's chapel downstairs. The chapel was situated on the eastern portion of the bottom flat of the men's dormitory. I joined the gathering and felt a measure of joy and satisfaction at being in the company of men with similar aspirations. The setting of the room evoked feelings of appreciation for God's presence and a desire for lofty ideals. The men sang robustly to the accompaniment of a piano. This was followed by words of welcome, special music, and study of that day's lesson from the Adult Sabbath School Quarterly.

As the facilitator expounded on the lesson, students interjected with their points of view on the subject under discussion. A lively discussion ensued that seemed to be never-ending. As one student after another chimed in, the course of the study vacillated. No one seemed eager to leave the chapel. The lesson study was still being elaborated on by pairs of students or larger groups of men when the presenter was reminded that it was almost time for breakfast in the college cafeteria. The closing exercises, which included prayer, were concluded and the men either headed to the cafeteria or hurried to their rooms before proceeding to the cafeteria for breakfast.

As we filed into the cafeteria, the day's lesson was still very much on our minds and many of us continued discussing it, sometimes heatedly. I, nonetheless, enjoyed this degree of enthusiasm and preoccupation with "holy things."

After breakfast I returned to the dorm, and the dean of men showed me to my assigned room. I gathered my few belongings and moved into my new room. The dean then introduced me to my roommates and briefed me on the activities that were to ensue later in the day.

I soon learned that the major activity scheduled for that day was registration for the fall quarter. The prospect of actually registering for classes at Caribbean Union College gave me a feeling of accomplishment.

I went to the Chapel Hall where the registration activities were being staged, collected my registration package, and began to look at the possible courses I would register for that quarter.

Before I left Guyana, my intention was to complete a double degree in theology and mathematics. However, the college did not have a full undergraduate program in mathematics. While going through my registration package and engaging in informal discussions with other students, I discovered that among the new program offerings that year was an emphasis in health ministry within the theology program. This immediately caught my attention.

At some time in the past, I had entertained a desire to pursue a career in medicine. I had even gone as far as importing various textbooks on medicine, including a medical dictionary. However, circumstances did not afford me the opportunity of pursuing medical training. And now, even though I longed to study mathematics at the degree level, the health ministry option within the theology program seemed a good alternative. I, therefore, decided to discuss this prospect with my academic adviser during my meeting with him later that morning.

During the meeting with my adviser, I outlined to him my study plans. I discussed with him the advisability of pursuing the health emphasis option

Thy Will Be Done

within the theology program. To my delight, I got the go ahead to pursue that option.

I began the registration process; however, I was unable to complete it that day. Before completing registration, I needed to convince the business manager that I would be able to take care of the expenses not covered by my tuition scholarship award.

I spent the better part of the afternoon searching for a job on campus. As I did so, I realized that doors of opportunity were few. Just at the point when I was about to give up my search for the day, I met a Guyanese pastor who had studied at Caribbean Union College several years earlier. I explained to him that I was having a difficult time finding an on-campus job. After some reflection, he advised that I try my luck at the Maintenance Department, so I got directions to that department and went to see the supervisor.

During my interview with the supervisor, I was asked what skills I could bring to the job. I proudly outlined to the supervisor that I had served a successful apprenticeship as a general building construction worker in Guyana after completing high school and had worked with my father in the shipwright industry, in addition to farming for most of my life. I assured him that I was capable of making a worthwhile contribution to the Maintenance Department.

I was overjoyed when the supervisor, Josephus Gilbert, affixed his signature to my registration form signifying that I had been offered part-time student employment in that department. I thanked God for working things out for me in this regard.

Early the next morning I hurried off to complete my registration. I began work and classes the following day. I was now on my way to fulfilling my long-standing ambition of becoming a minister.

I launched into my study program at CUC with lots of enthusiasm and high expectations. The novelty of this early college experience motivated me to do my best. By the end of the first quarter, I had settled into college life quite nicely. The college church elected me as a deacon and a leader for the Adventist Youth Department. I was also elected sergeant-at-arms of the Spartans Men's Club. That first quarter I also made the honor roll and received a certificate of excellence for outstanding academic achievement.

I did not receive any substantial financial assistance from home due to foreign exchange restrictions. Thus, in order to meet my financial obligations, I had to lean heavily on the Lord. God provided financial assistance for me in a variety of ways, including assistance from friends and off-campus work.

Some mornings, like Jesus did, I would get up before daybreak and go to the chapel or some secluded spot on campus to pour out my heart to God on a variety of challenges I was facing at school. Sometimes, without knowing it, when I opened my eyes I found other students similarly engaged in seeking the Lord's guidance through prayer. Whenever I returned from those sessions of communing with God, I felt refreshed and equipped to face the challenges before me.

Though already at college, I still wondered about the outcome of my application to the Inter-American Development Bank for a scholarship to study at the University of Guyana that same year. During the latter part of my first quarter of studies, I received word from the IDB that I had been awarded a grant to study mathematics full time at the University of Guyana for the 1988-89 academic year. My reaction to the news was mixed. If I had received that approval of funding before that of the Guyana Conference, things would have been quite different. I would have still been in Guyana and well on my way to completing my degree in mathematics. But at that point in my life, God had made known His will for my life in no uncertain terms through His providential workings. Being at CUC at that time was His will for me, and in spite of how appealing the option of studying mathematics at the University of Guyana was, I resolved to stay within the orbit of God's revealed will for my life at that time.

Notwithstanding, I wrote and thanked the agency for favorably considering my request for funding. I also informed them that my plans had changed that year as far as continuing my studies at the University of Guyana was concerned and that I was not in a position to utilize the study grant. I indicated that I might be in a position to accept their offer at a future date.

Although it was hard to believe, the end of first quarter was quickly approaching. My study program was moving apace. Added to my other extracurricular activities, I joined the college choir where I sang baritone and bass. At the final meeting of the Guyanese Club that year, I was nominated president.

Towards the end of the 1988-89 school year, CUC instituted an early registration system whereby students were required to register for classes for the ensuing quarter by the end of the previous quarter. Consequently, toward the end of the fall quarter registration began for the winter quarter.

When it was my turn to register, I had some forebodings. Even though I received some earnings from my part-time job on campus, I still owed the college a substantial sum of money for living expenses. Based on my discussions with senior students, CUC had very stringent rules regarding paying of fees.

Several students told me that because I owed such a large sum of money to the college there was no way I would be allowed to register under the prevailing circumstances. To be able to register, I needed to first clear off my arrears and at least make a down payment on my fees for the ensuing quarter.

Thy Will Be Done

On the day of registration, I prayed earnestly to God to grant me favor with all those officers with whom I would be coming in contact during the registration process. The preliminary aspects of the registration procedure progressed quite smoothly. Then the time came for me to receive clearance from the director of student finance. As I took my seat at her desk, I whispered a prayer to God for a favorable response from this officer. As she began checking through my registration papers, she seemed inclined to allow me to register. However, when she came to the financial section of the form where she was required to affix her signature, she paused, lifted her head, peered at me over her glasses, and said, "Alexander, I see here that you have a large balance currently owing to the college."

"I am aware of that fact."

"How much money do you have on hand?"

"I do not have any money currently." As I spoke, I prayed in my heart for God to guide me in my response.

"Alexander, you will need to clear off your outstanding balance before you will be allowed to register for next quarter. You see, even though you are a tuition scholarship recipient, you still need to find some cash to take care of your living expenses for each quarter of your studies."

"I am fully aware of my current financial obligations to the school, but I do not have any money at this time. Actually, I had hoped by this point to acquire enough work credits from student labor to clear off my existing debit to the college as well as be in a position to make a deposit toward next quarter's living expenses."

"I understand, but I cannot register you for next quarter until you come up with the finances. You need to come up with some money."

As I lingered in her presence my mind began to race. It appeared as though all the efforts expended on my studies and this whole notion about attending CUC were about to come to a grinding halt. I thought through the situation, quickly. "I would like to meet with the Business Manager and present my case to him."

"That is not possible! He will not meet with you."

As I walked away from her desk, I resolved to take my case to the next level by seeking an audience with the business manager of the college notwithstanding the director of student finance's dissuasion. So I went to his office and requested a meeting with him. His secretary told me to go ahead and knock on his office door.

After knocking, I heard him say, "Come in please."

"Good morning, Mr. St. Hilare."

"Good morning. Have a seat please. How can I help you?"

"I am here to speak to you about my financial obligations to CUC and seek your help so that I can register for the next quarter."

"Let me hear what you have to say."

"Well, sir, I am a Guyanese student studying theology here on campus. I am a tuition scholarship recipient from the Guyana Conference of SDA. However, due to financial constraints, I currently owe the school some money for the current quarter and am not in a position to clear that off at this point nor make a deposit toward next quarter's fees." I braced myself for what would come next.

"How much do you owe the school?"

"I cannot remember exactly."

"Go to the director of student finance and ask her to send me your file."

"Okay, sir."

I hurried out of his office and made my way back to the director of student finance. When I told her what the business manager had said, she seemed surprised that I had actually gotten an audience with him. However, she gave me my file, and I returned to the business manager's office immediately.

I cannot remember what the outstanding amount was, but after I handed my file over to him, he glanced at the contents, looked me in the eye and said, "How do you plan to pay off this outstanding balance?"

"I plan to do so by continuing working at my part-time job here on campus and working full time throughout the Christmas vacation."

As I spoke, I saw a half half-smile cross his face and he said, "Alexander, even if you work full time during the Christmas holidays, you will still not be able to clear off your balance and make enough to go toward next quarter's tuition."

There was a moment of silence, then he continued. "You know, Alexander, contrary to what people say about this college, we reward people who contribute toward this institution. Whenever I look through my office windows or drive about campus, I see you at work faithfully cutting the lawns. This college rewards people who are diligent." Little did I realize that I was being watched as I discharged my duties.

He continued, "I am willing to help you. I want you to sit right here in my office and put in writing what you just told me about how you plan to clear off your current expenses."

I did as I was told, and within a short while, I passed the written agreement over to him.

"Where is your registration procedure sheet?"

"Here it is, sir."

Thy Will Be Done

"Give it to me."

I handed it to him, and he affixed his signature, thereby authorizing me to register for classes for the ensuing quarter. As he returned the form to me he said, "Take this back to the director of student finance and complete your registration."

"Thank you very much, Mr. St. Hilare."

"You're welcome! Good luck to you."

I thanked God for once again working things out in my favor. At that point, two passages of Scripture came to mind. The first was, "Seest thou a man diligent in his business? he shall stand before kings; he shall not stand before mean men" (Prov. 22:29). The second was, "Whatsoever thy hand findeth to do, do it with thy might; for there is no work, nor device, nor knowledge, nor wisdom, in the grave, wither thou goest" (Eccl. 9:10).

I hurried to the director's desk and told her that the business manager had cleared me for registration. I handed her the signed registration procedure sheet and my agreement. She then stamped my registration form and issued to me my financial clearance so that I could complete the registration process.

Within a matter of half an hour thereafter, I had completed registration. As I walked out of the registration room, my heart was overflowing with gratitude to God for the way things had gone. My heart was put at ease on this matter, and I was able to focus my mind on my studies for the remainder of the quarter.

When the first quarter ended, most of the students returned home for the Christmas holidays. I had hoped to be back in Guyana for the Christmas holidays, but with my financial situation as it was, I had to give up any thought of returning to Guyana for Christmas. Besides, I had indicated to the business manager that I would work full time during the Christmas break. I, therefore, sought to honor my word in that regard.

A few days before Christmas all the departments closed for the holiday. Fortunately, several students remained on campus. But although I had company, I missed home so much. I cried more than once during the break. It was the first time I had been away from home for that long. Moreover, it was the first time I had been away from home for Christmas.

The college made arrangements for students who remained on campus to spend Christmas day with the faculty and staff in their homes. On Christmas morning I had breakfast at a faculty home. Then at lunchtime several of us were guests at another faculty member's home where we had a sumptuous lunch. There was a wide variety of delicacies to be enjoyed. I made the best of that special opportunity to feast at the banquet table as it were. For supper I returned to the faculty member's home where I had breakfast. The social interaction

A New Beginning

experienced at each mealtime was rich and enjoyable. It felt like a home away from home. Remaining on campus was not too bad after all.

The Christmas vacation came and went, and it was soon time to begin the second quarter. During that quarter I made some great strides in my school work in addition to keeping up with my extracurricular activities.

I had many friends on campus, including members of the opposite sex, but I had developed a special interest in a young woman back in Guyana before leaving for CUC. However, we had not committed to a long term relationship before I left for college. I was intentionally being very cautious not to build her hopes up and then have them dashed as had been the experience of a number of my friends in the past. During the Christmas break, through God's providential workings, and a train of events, we committed to a special friendship.

By God's providence, I was able to register for classes for the third quarter even though I still had some outstanding bills at the school. I continued to work hard at my studies and my part-time jobs.

At the close of the school year, I still owed the college approximately TT$2,000. Therefore, as the summer vacation got underway, I was preoccupied with trying to clear off my outstanding balance as well as earning enough to at least see me through the fall quarter of the new school year. Toward that end, I had to find some means of securing enough employment during the summer to generate the funds needed. I prayed earnestly for God's intervention and provision in that regard.

I decided to sign up for full-time work in the Maintenance Department. By my calculations, if I worked full time in that department throughout the summer, I would be able to defray my outstanding expenses at the college. But it did not seem likely that I would be able to earn anything extra from that source to go toward my registration for the fall quarter of the ensuing school year. What should I do? Moreover, what would God do on my behalf this time around?

One evening during the early weeks of summer a student from Guyana approached me and inquired about my willingness to teach the mathematics and science modules to four young men from the United States who were preparing to write the General Education Development (GED) examination. These men were aspiring to enter the aviation school in Trinidad to be trained as pilots to work with the national airline of Trinidad and Tobago, British West Indian Airways (BWIA), subsequently renamed Caribbean Airlines. Time was of the essence in this regard, and the men were willing to pay for the tutoring in preparation for the examinations. The Lord was opening up another door of opportunity for me to be able to earn some much-needed income.

Dr. Elvin Gabriel, the academic dean of CUC, had mentioned this prospect

Thy Will Be Done

to my friend and asked for recommendations of suitable persons to prepare the students for the examination. My friend, Mark Austin, agreed to teach English, history, and social studies, and I agreed to teach mathematics and science.

In order to complete the syllabus in a month's time, I was required to devote two evenings per week from 5:30-7:30 p.m. to teaching. That meant that after I got off work at 5:15 p.m., I had to hurry to the dormitory to tidy up, grab my notes, and proceed to class.

Toward the end of the GED training course with the pilots, I learned that there were vacancies for security guards to work on campus. Having served previously in Guyana as a teacher officer with the Guyana National Service (GNS), a paramilitary organization, I felt confident of executing the duties that would be required of me as a security guard. I, therefore, applied and was accepted for employment as a security guard for the night shifts. Here again was another means the Lord had placed in my path for earning money for college.

When the GED classes ended, I began working with the campus Security Department. Working at a full-time job from 7:15 a.m. to 5:15 p.m. Monday through Thursday and 7:15 to noon on Friday, and as a security guard on one of the night shifts, turned out to be very demanding. Further, there were several instances when a security guard did not show up for his particular shift. In such cases, I had to work the other shift, which ended at 6:00 a.m. the following morning. On such occasions, after coming off that particular shift, I headed straight for the cafeteria to have my breakfast before running off to my full-time job that started at 7:15 a.m.

During the spring quarter of the 1988-89 school year, Mrs. Shirley McGarrell joined the faculty and moved to CUC. As the summer months approached, she asked me to stay at her home on campus during the summer along with another student while she returned to the United States to complete moving arrangements. I readily accepted the offer as it meant I would not have to pay any dormitory fees that summer.

By the end of summer I had liquidated my debt to the college and had a credit balance of $200 on my account. At that point, I had no idea of where the additional funding would come from for me to register for classes for the fall quarter, but based on God's providential workings on my behalf in the past, I decided to trust Him to provide for me once more.

Up until a few days before registration, I had not gotten any breakthrough regarding financial support for the ensuing quarter. One evening, while in casual conversation with some Guyanese friends, one of them mentioned that there was an opening in the CUC high school for a mathematics and science student teacher.

The high school had already opened for classes for that term when one of the mathematics and science teachers resigned her position to take up a teaching appointment on another Caribbean island. The school's administration needed to fill the vacant position as soon as possible. The person they were looking for to fill the vacancy needed to be able to teach mathematics at the junior and senior levels, teach integrated science in the junior high department and biology in the middle school department. Knowing that I was a trained secondary school mathematics and science teacher, my friend encouraged me to apply for the vacant position.

At first, I did not take him seriously. However, as I turned this prospect over in my mind, I reasoned that there was no harm in at least filling out an application for the position. Besides, the timing seemed just right. I viewed myself as a candidate who had the exact qualifications required to fill the vacancy. Moreover, I thought that maybe this was God's way of giving me a break that would be a means of helping me to fund my education at CUC for the remainder of my time there. Further, operating from the premise, "In the morning sow thy seed, and in the evening withhold not thine hand: for thou knowest not whether shall prosper, either this or that, or whether they both shall be alike good" (Eccl. 11:6), I submitted an application the following day.

Within two days of turning in my application, I received a telephone call from the college president, Dr. Vernon Andrews, inviting me to an interview. I reasoned that this was a sure sign that my application was at least being given some consideration. As far as I knew then, I was the only trained teacher of mathematics on campus, and I thought that I stood a good chance of being picked to fill the vacancy. Imagine my joy and excitement at the prospect of actually working as a student teacher at the high school on campus. This would mean no more toiling in the hot sun mowing the lawns on campus. I could hardly wait for the outcome of the interview.

The following morning I asked for time off from my job at the Maintenance Department and presented myself for the interview at the president's office. The president briefed me about the position and what it would demand of me.

"When I saw your application for the position, I wondered if it was the same person who cut the lawns on campus. Seeing you now answers my question. Why didn't you apply for a teaching job on campus before? Normally, a person with your kind of qualifications would have sought a student job commensurate with his or her training and experience. But there you are, working diligently as a grounds man."

"I did not see the need to do so before, Sir. My motto in life is to do my best at whatever task I am assigned."

"Alexander, taking into consideration your academic and professional preparation, we believe that you are the best candidate to fill the vacancy in the high school. We would, therefore, like to offer you the position."

I was elated, surprised, and thankful all at once. Elated because my application was considered from among many other applicants; surprised because I did not expect things to work themselves out so easily; and thankful because that was what I had prayed for and God had answered in such a prompt and remarkable way.

"In return for your services, we are offering you a package that includes free on-campus housing, a monthly income, as well as a two-year tuition scholarship for the last two years of your study program here at CUC."

This was more than I had bargained for! I had to really control my emotions at that point because, rather than waiting for the president to ask me to make a decision on the offer, I felt like volunteering my acceptance right at that moment. However, I managed to wait it out lest I be perceived as being over anxious.

Dr. Andrews continued, "I would like you to consider the offer and let me know as soon as possible what your decision is in this regard. Do you have any questions for me?"

"Yes, Dr. Andrews. Let's suppose that I choose to accept the position, when will I be expected to begin working?"

"The appointment will begin soon after you signal your acceptance of the offer. The ball is now in your court."

"Okay, sir. I will get back to you on this by tomorrow."

I walked out of the president's office in high spirits. I felt as though I was walking on air. My mind raced. I could hardly believe my good fortunes. This was much more than I had anticipated. I was convinced that this was the mighty hand of God at work in my life once more, and I thanked Him for it over and over again.

On my way back to the McGarrell's residence on campus where I was staying, I reasoned that this offer could well signal the end of my manual labor on the campus grounds, even though I enjoyed my job.

However, a few questions were foremost in my mind. First, how would I make the transition from working as a laborer on the grounds to a teacher in the classroom? Second, how would my supervisor react to the news of my resignation from my current job? This was even more worrying since I was the only one working on grounds at that time, and my supervisor had just bought a new lawn mower to enhance my work with the department. *Will they find someone with the same degree of dedication and diligence to fill the vacancy that*

A New Beginning

will be created on account of my departure? I worried.

When I finally got to my room, I knelt down and offered a prayer of thanksgiving to God for His blessing in such a great way by putting me in the stream of His providence. From my standpoint, this offer was too good to be turned down. I had already accepted it in my mind. Notwithstanding, I asked God to show me if, in His view, I should accept the offer.

I shared the news of the job offer with a few close friends, and they all encouraged me to accept it.

The following morning I made this a matter of prayer once more during my devotion. When I got up from my knees, I felt assured that God had sanctioned my decision to accept the offer. I surmised that I had nothing to lose and much to gain by accepting it. Besides, God had not indicated anything to the contrary. There was no time to lose. I decided to communicate my acceptance of the offer to the college president that same morning.

At around midmorning, I asked for some time off from my job so that I could visit the president's office and communicate my acceptance of the offer in person.

After I arrived at the president's office I was ushered into his presence by his Administrative Assistant. Once seated I began, "Good morning Dr. Andrews."

"Good morning Alexander."

"I am here to let you know my decision regarding your job offer." He sat up in his chair and waited for me to continue.

"After giving the offer careful and prayerful consideration, I have decided to accept it."

"That's great, Alexander."

His words and demeanor signaled his satisfaction with my decision. He told me to report to Dr. Benjamin Igwee, the principal of the high school, immediately and make arrangements for assumption of duties. As I prepared to leave his office, Dr. Andrews encouraged me to give of my best at my new job. I pledged to do so wholeheartedly.

By the time I arrived at the high school principal's office, I realized that Dr. Andrews had already called him to communicate the outcome of the interview. After exchanging a few pleasantries, Dr. Igwee advised that I begin duties the following day. When I walked out of his office, I felt a strong sense of gratitude to God for the outworking of His providence in my life once again.

I informed the maintenance supervisor about the job offer and that I had to report for duties the following morning. Contrary to my earlier fears, the supervisor readily granted me release from my job and encouraged me to do

Thy Will Be Done

my best. He wished me every success in my new appointment.

The Lord had come through for me again. But this time around, He had done so beyond my wildest dreams, and I was truly grateful.

The following morning I showed up for work at the secondary school, neatly dressed. The principal assigned me my teaching load and I was introduced to the first class that I would be teaching that morning.

When I walked into the classroom and was introduced as the new mathematics teacher, the students muttered under their breath. In addition, there were unwelcoming glances from some of them. I began to feel uneasy.

Before beginning my first lesson, I introduced myself to the class in a more personal and detailed way. I told them, among other things, of my professional training in mathematics and science at the college and university levels. After learning that I was a trained mathematics specialist teacher and that I had completed one year of undergraduate mathematics study at the University of Guyana, the students were somewhat reassured and seemed more eager to give me their attention than when I had first entered the classroom.

I have reason enough to believe that part of the reason for the uneasiness shown by the students stemmed from the fact that they had grown accustomed to seeing me working on the grounds cutting the lawn. Showing up as their new mathematics teacher did not seem to make much sense in their minds. They probably could not reconcile the fact that a person working on the grounds could be elevated to the rank of a specialist mathematics/science teacher overnight. As a matter of fact, the day before, I had actually mowed the grass around the high school. There was no way, in their reasoning, that a laborer could be a mathematics teacher in disguise. Notwithstanding the affront meted out to me by the students, I proceeded to teach my first mathematics lesson to the class.

I chose to be very deliberate and thorough as I moved through the lesson. About halfway through the lesson, the murmurings had decreased significantly and the students seemed to be absorbed with the lesson. By the end of the class, the students appeared to be on board with me. One of them actually came to my table as the students were filing out of the classroom and spoke in a subdued tone, "Sir, I think that you have done an excellent job at teaching your first lesson. You're off to a good start. Keep it up!" I felt encouraged by this remark and resolved to continue giving of my best in my teaching stint at the high school.

I really enjoyed teaching at the CUC high school. My experience at that school can be classified as one of my best teaching stints throughout my primary and secondary school teaching career. For the most part, the students were rather receptive to learning. Some of them exhibited extraordinary sharp

A New Beginning

academic acumen. My classroom teaching came alive, and it was evident that active learning was taking place. The students enjoyed my teaching style so much that they referred to me fondly as "Sir Maths."

At the end of my first year of teaching, my students did very well at the regional Caribbean Examinations Council (CXC) examinations. I remember one parent who, on learning of her daughter's success at the mathematics examination, pulled up at the school, got out of her car, and, in jubilation, literally ran down a slope, almost falling headlong into me, and thanked me for helping her daughter succeed at the examinations. After that, she reposed such confidence in my teaching ability that she subsequently requested a transfer of her younger daughter to my mathematics class so that I could prepare her for the CXC mathematics examinations the following year. To her parents' delight, and my obvious satisfaction, this second daughter passed the CXC mathematics examination with a distinction when she wrote it the following year.

In addition to my teaching load at the high school, the college president asked me to take on the additional responsibility of tutoring college students who were enrolled in the bachelor of business administration degree program but needed a pass in mathematics at the CXC General Proficiency level to fulfill the admission requirements for their program major.

These college students also did extremely well at the CXC mathematics examinations the following year. This was also cause for great joy and celebration among the students, faculty, and staff of the college.

On account of the success achieved by the students under my tutelage, the college willingly agreed to renew my contract for another year. The success rate of my students continued year after year. And each year my contract was renewed without any difficulty.

I attribute the success achieved during my teaching stint to hard work; adequate preparation for each class; my academic preparation, especially my specialized training in mathematics at the teacher training college; my one year of studies in the bachelor's degree program in mathematics at the University of Guyana; the students' willingness and eagerness to learn; my love for the subject; maintaining a good rapport with the students; and, above all, the blessings of God.

I cherish the fond memories of my interactions with students who blossomed under my instruction at the CUC high school. Many of them have since gone on to achieve higher education and advanced degrees. Whenever I come across some of them, they remind me of how I encouraged them along the way. Many thank me profusely for my role in their educational lives. These disclosures give me a great degree of satisfaction.

During my years at Caribbean Union College, I experienced growth in my

Thy Will Be Done

Christian, academic, and social life. Under my leadership, the Guyanese Club grew and became more vibrant. Our programs were so appealing that every Saturday night a large number of non-Guyanese nationals were in attendance. The Guyanese Club staged many campus events that left indelible impressions on the minds of students and faculty alike. The club also hosted many off-campus activities, the most significant one being an outing to the island of Tobago, during the 1990 Easter break.

As CUC's social activities coordinator for two consecutive years, I planned a wide array of activities for faculty and students alike. On select Saturday nights, I organized hikes up the Maracas Valley. Students, faculty, and staff looked forward to those hikes. On most occasions a major hike was planned early in the school year as a means of getting the students and faculty acquainted with each other. On such a hike, I would put the participants in pairs before moving off. Along the way, the pairs were asked to strike up a conversation with each other for a specified period of time. At the sound of my whistle, each pair was required to switch places with the pair either in front of them or behind them. By repeating this action a number of times throughout the one-hour hike, it was hoped that each individual would have gotten a chance to meet several persons for the first time.

Interestingly enough, the major challenge faced by the organizers of the hike was getting individuals to change partners along the way. In a number of instances, once the pairs became engaged in a conversation, they seldom obeyed the command to switch partners at the sound of the whistle. As I walked back down the line and encouraged people to obey the whistle, I saw several of the male students in particular trying to get in some last point or squeeze something more than a casual acquaintance out of the conversation. The female counterparts, too, did not seem to resist such overtures. As a matter of fact, after the hike was over, many permanent relationships developed.

My degree of involvement and responsibility in the Ministerial Association on campus grew each year to the extent that during my final year I was elected president of the association. Each year the association staged a retreat that everyone anticipated. At the retreat experienced church leaders and mentors discussed and presented on matters relating to ministry. The association also sought to inculcate in ministerial students values such as integrity, self-respect, moral soundness, an exemplary way of life that spoke of the students' walk with Christ, and service as Christian ambassadors in the cause of humanity. This was reinforced particularly by faculty in the Theology Department, many of whom were themselves former pastors, conference administrators, and departmental directors. This proved to be rather enriching.

A New Beginning

At CUC I had numerous opportunities to sharpen my preaching skills. I secured quite a number of preaching appointments on and off campus. And when there was an opportunity for me to share the good news about Jesus, I took advantage of it. Consequently, I was invited to preach at events on Sabbath, Sunday night, Wednesday night, and at special events at a number of churches across Trinidad and Tobago.

With the help of the Holy Spirit, my messages got across to the listening audiences. I remember quite vividly when, on one occasion, after I preached at a Community Guest Day at one of the churches in Trinidad, I made an appeal for people to give their lives to Jesus. Many individuals responded to my call and came to the altar. One lady motioned to me that she wanted to have a brief word with me after the service. I agreed to meet her in the vestry. As we made our way toward the vestry, I got the feeling that many eyes were watching us. Brushing aside those stares, I met with the woman as requested. She startled me somewhat when she disclosed to me very early in our discourse that she had been a harlot for many years. She told me that during the sermon the Holy Spirit had convicted her and she wanted to surrender her life fully to Jesus Christ. I encouraged her to follow through with her decision. After praying with her, I spoke with the church leadership and recommended that the Bible worker, incidentally a female, be assigned to guide this woman through a series of Bible studies in preparation for baptism.

On another occasion while preaching at a Community Guest Day at another church, one of the parishioners came up to me after the sermon and said, "Brother, thanks for the message you preached this morning. I was richly blessed by it. God used you mightily today. Keep it up! May He continue to bless you richly in your studies and subsequent ministry. You must invite me to your graduation. It will be a distinct honor for me to see you march down the aisle at graduation as a ministerial graduate."

On Friday afternoons the dormitory students had to tidy their rooms in preparation for Sabbath. At a certain time during the course of the afternoon, the deans of the two dormitories went around and inspected each room. Points were awarded for such things as tidiness, creativity, neatness, ambience, and overall general appearance. During the preparation for inspection, recorded sermons of some of the great preachers in Adventism, including Henry Wright, Richard (Dick) Baron, Walter Pearson, Charles E. Bradford, Alvin Kibble, Barry L. Black, Charles Brooks, and some from other denominations could be heard streaming from the rooms. Those were really inspirational moments. A similar scenario could be observed on Friday evenings after vespers as well as on Sabbath afternoons.

Thy Will Be Done

Another spiritual high on campus was the quarterly Week of Prayer. During those weeks, preachers of renown were invited to campus as guest speakers. Those sessions left indelible impressions on my mind and inspired me to keep traveling down the path I was on. Those types of events also reinforced my call to the ministry and gave me the impetus to continue giving of my best in my studies as I prepared to take up this divine calling.

During my final year, as part of my Ministerial Practicum class, I was able to gain a glimpse of what full-time ministry would be like. A number of fellow classmates and I were engaged in a crusade in Acono, a little village on the outskirts of CUC. Each night a different preacher presented the message. God blessed our efforts with twenty-six baptisms.

In addition to my practicum, I carried a class load of eighteen credits and continued teaching at the high school. Furthermore, I was elected president of the graduating class of 1992. That year, I served as president of the Guyanese Club, president of the Ministerial Association, and a member of the Social Committee simultaneously. The Lord truly helped me accomplish all of these activities. The glory and praise belong to Him.

After four years of study at Caribbean Union College, I graduated with a bachelor's degree in theology with an emphasis in health ministry. Such an achievement filled me with a sense of accomplishment. How I managed to achieve so much during my stay at CUC still boggles my mind. God had indeed "borne me on eagle's wings" throughout my sojourn there and that made the difference.

After graduation, I did not return to Guyana immediately. At that time, I was preparing a group of students to write the CXC General Proficiency examinations the following year, and they persuaded me to stay on at CUC for an additional year and see them through to the examinations. After giving the matter serious thought, I gave in to the students' request.

For each quarter of that additional year at CUC, I was privileged to complete a maximum of eight credits free of charge. I chose my courses very carefully. The courses I studied during that period supplemented my health ministry emphasis by exposing me to courses in pastoral ministry which I did not study as part of my health ministry major. I was also sure to take the prerequisite courses essential to my acceptance into and success at graduate level studies in public health.

The year 1992 ended on a high note when, on December 20, I married my fiancé, Andrea Nelson. We honeymooned on the beautiful island of Tobago, the twin island of Trinidad. After our honeymoon was over, I continued my teaching stint at the high school while my wife returned to Guyana.

A New Beginning

When the 1992-93 academic year was nearing its end, on account of the success I had achieved during my teaching career at the CUC high school, I was offered a number of teaching jobs in Trinidad as well as on other Caribbean islands. As attractive and lucrative as those offers were, I decided to return to Guyana after my students wrote the CXC examinations. Notwithstanding the fact that I was a trained teacher and could attract a decent salary in exchange for my services, I viewed my involvement in teaching on the campus as a means to an end and not an end in itself. Therefore, I chose to return to Guyana toward the end of August, just before the CXC results were out lest I be persuaded to continue in the teaching profession for an extended period of time once the results were out. The time had come for me to make full proof of my ministry, and I was very anxious to begin serving the Lord as a minister of the gospel. I shipped my meager belongings and returned to Guyana to a job opening that was awaiting me at the Guyana Conference of Seventh-day Adventists.

Within seven days of returning to Guyana, the CXC results were out. And from the reports received, many of my students had done very well once more. I was encouraged to return to CUC and continue offering my services at the secondary school, but I stuck with my decision to begin my pastoral ministry within the Guyana Conference.

Chapter 17

Making Full Proof of My Ministry

Within a few days of arriving in Guyana, I reported to the president of the Guyana Conference of Seventh-day Adventists, Pastor Hilton Garnett.

During my audience with the president I learned that, the conference administration was giving consideration to assigning me to the West Demerara pastoral district. As the discussion progressed, I made a cursory remark to the president that my theological training at CUC included a health ministries component, virtually a second major, and that I was willing to offer my public health expertise to the constituency simultaneously with my pastoral assignment if my services were needed.

Interestingly, Pastor Garnett informed me that the conference administration was currently looking for someone with a strong public health background to head the Health Ministries Department of the Conference. My pastoral assignment was deferred for the time being. The Conference Executive Committee was scheduled to meet within a few days. When I left the president's office, I prayed that God would have His way and that His will would be done. I kept praying during the ensuing days leading up to the committee meeting.

The Executive Committee voted in favor of my appointment as health ministries director. They also voted that I begin my ministerial internship in the Georgetown Number 2 District under Pastor Keith Drakes.

I began working immediately. My prior exposure to church leadership as an ordained elder in my local church, coupled with my exposure to and service in the various auxiliary departments in the church prior to studying at CUC came in handy. As challenging as ministry was, I was able to integrate my work at the office with pastoral work in the district in a unique way.

During the week, special days were assigned for visitation of church members . The visitation team comprised of Pastor Drakes, district pastor; Brother Clarence Webster, the district Bible worker; and myself. At other times Brother Webster and I went alone. Also, on a number of occasions, I did visitation on my own.

On Sabbaths I had preaching appointments at the churches. In the afternoons I traveled to different districts and conducted training programs for health secretaries in the churches. Other health ministry training programs were conducted on the weekend, primarily on Sundays.

There was a lot of work to be done to revive the Health and Temperance Department of the conference to make it viable once more. I, therefore, got to work organizing and conducting training programs in the districts and conducting seminars and community health outreach activities in a number of villages.

A number of health parades and rallies, as well as fitness walks and runs were staged. I also fostered the formation of health clubs in the churches, organized Health Ministries Councils, and instituted a local chapter of the Adventist Health Professionals Association, among other activities. Simultaneously, I sought to forge relationships with other faith-based organizations, government ministries, and the Health Ministries Department of the Caribbean Union and the Inter-American Division, respectively.

Within a few months of beginning my work assignment with the conference, the Health Ministries Department was up and running once more.

I enjoyed my work in pastoral and health ministry a whole lot. It was so satisfying to see lives changed through the preaching of the Gospel and to see people living healthier lives.

I sought to minister to the needs of the whole congregation, catering to the needs of young and old alike so much so that I was often referred to as a "congregational" pastor. There was much to learn from the membership, and I always availed myself of such learning opportunities.

My first exposure to managing a large evangelistic campaign came in 1995 when a US-based Guyanese pastor, Fitzroy Jackson, conducted a citywide crusade titled "The Gospel in TechniColor."

The crusade was held in North Ruimveldt, and I was tasked with the responsibility of managing it. With the help of God and the dedicated work of the team members, after four weeks of nightly meetings, 187 individuals took their stand for Jesus Christ and were baptized. God be praised!

With the passage of time, I matured into a successful and productive pastor. It was evident that God was leading in my life and was blessing my ministry with success. Wherever and whenever I would meet members after serving in a particular church or district, they greeted me openly and showed me the respect befitting of the ministry.

In 1995, after the resignation of the country director of the Adventist Development and Relief Agency (ADRA), the conference appointed me ADRA

Thy Will Be Done

Guyana Country Director. Serving with ADRA gave me an opportunity to meaningfully participate in, and foster the work of this development and relief arm of the Adventist Church.

After serving as ADRA Director for nine months, a new country director was hired, and I relinquished the position. But I resolved to undergo further specialized training in health, development, and relief to be better able to serve the church in the future should such an opportunity be afforded me.

My ardent efforts in the area of health ministries was recognized, and through the instrumentality of the Inter-American Division Health Ministries Director, Dr. Elie Honore, I was awarded a scholarship to pursue a four-month course of specialized training in public health nutrition, family life education, food preparation and demonstration, and religious studies at the Pacific Health Education Center in Bakersfield, California. The training I received through this program served to enhance my work in health ministries and whet my appetite for advanced training and work in public health.

At the Guyana Conference Session in August 1996, I was returned to office as health ministries director for another term. I was also elected communication director. Later on in the year, I was also named the Guyana Conference of Seventh-day Adventists pastoral representative on the Caribbean Union Conference Executive Committee. I learned a lot by attending the committee meetings. Serving in this capacity exposed me to some of the inner workings of the Seventh-day Adventist Church at the higher level.

In 1996 I was also assigned to the Georgetown Number 2 District in a joint pastoral leadership position with Pastor Clement Henry. During this stint we worked ardently to advance the work in that district.

The Lord continued to bless my ministry, and I felt that it was only a matter of time before I would be considered for ordination. However, the Lord had other plans for my life at that juncture.

Chapter 18

Providence at Work Again

Ever since studying theology and public health at Caribbean Union College, I harbored the desire to pursue graduate studies in public health. The public health courses studied during my undergraduate program at CUC, the practical applications made of my learning, and the potential for greater usefulness in the church as a public health specialist propelled me to seek out advanced training in public health.

In addition, the public health activities I had engaged in since returning to Guyana from CUC and serving as the health ministries director of the conference and country director for ADRA, coupled with the training at the Pacific Health Education Center served to enhance my desire for additional training in public health.

While in my third year at CUC, I had begun to seek out opportunities and avenues through which I could pursue graduate training in public health. I wrote several graduate schools and sought acceptance into a master of public health degree program.

In my search for a suitable course of study, two majors stood out, namely international health (now commonly referred to as global health) and health promotion and education. As I surveyed the course contents provided by the universities to which I had written, I surmised that these two majors would serve me well in my future work for the church. The program course offerings for the international health major seemed well suited to international health and development kinds of work akin to what was being done through ADRA, while the health promotion and education major course offerings were more suited for health and temperance work. Further, the international health major included a number of courses that were similar to the field of primary health care. I, therefore, concluded that since it was unlikely that I would be pursuing a medical degree after all, a master's in public health in international health was the nearest I could get to the study of medicine, which had been one of my earlier ambitions.

Even though all the universities I had written to had really impressive programs in either international health or health promotion and education,

Thy Will Be Done

Loma Linda University was the only school that offered a double major in these two disciplines within the master's of public health program offerings. *If only I could get the opportunity to complete both programs simultaneously,* I thought, *that would be ideal.*

By the time I had graduated from CUC, I had gained acceptance into four prestigious universities in the United States, namely Columbia University, Tulane University, the University of North Carolina-Chapel Hill, and Loma Linda University. Even though I was very zealous in my efforts to pursue graduate studies, my major constraint was finances.

As a consequence of not having the required deposit to enroll at three of those universities, I forfeited my offer of a place in their program. Loma Linda was willing to keep me on record as a prospective student provided I kept my student status current each year by applying for a deferral.

As it turned out, a one-year deferral ended up being three years in a row. Each year I wrote the Director of Admissions at Loma Linda University School of Public Health and asked for another year's deferral. With my acceptance deferred over the next several years, I continued to seek out avenues through which I could secure funding for my intended study program at that institution.

In 1995, while undergoing specialized training at Pacific Health Education Center, I was privileged to visit Loma Linda University and receive a tour of the facility firsthand. I was impressed with what I saw and was further inspired to attend that institution of higher learning. Merely walking the grounds of Loma Linda University was deemed a special privilege. I met with university officials, including the dean of the School of Public Health. Being a student at Loma Linda University would be a delight for me, and I cherished the thought that one day that desire might be realized. But when that would be, I could not say.

While meeting with Dr. Richard Hart, the dean of the School of Public Health, I asked about university funding to pursue studies leading to the award of a master's degree in public health. According to him, there were hundreds of similar requests from students at any given point in time, and the university had very limited funding for scholarships. While on campus, I took the opportunity to defer my acceptance for another year.

I continued seeking out avenues of possible funding for my study program at Loma Linda University. At that time, the cost of tuition for one year with a course load of twelve credits was more than US$13,000. When living expenses such as room and board and utilities for a family of three and the cost of textbooks were factored in, the figure rose to somewhere around US$25,000. Thus, my anticipated two-year study program would require at least an investment of US$50,000. Then there was the US$3,000 deposit required of each international student before even arriving on campus, and of course there was insurance and the cost of traveling to Loma Linda. From a personal standpoint, all of these costs were prohibitive. However, I consoled myself with the fact that if it was God's will that I study at Loma Linda University, He would make a way somehow.

While I began exploring possible sources of funding to pursue graduate studies in public health, I came across the Organization of American States (OAS), an agency that provides funding opportunities in the form of fellowships to students from member countries of the OAS. However, in order for an individual to receive funding, his or her home country had to be a full member of the OAS. At the time when I first came across the OAS, Guyana was an associate member of that body. Guyanese nationals were therefore not entitled to funding through the organization's fellowship program at that time.

With the passage of time, I made it my duty to follow closely Guyana's progress toward the attainment of full membership status with the OAS. I determined that once Guyana became a full member, I would apply for a scholarship.

One evening in 1996 I could hardly believe my ears when I heard over one of our news channels that Guyana had been voted as a full member of the OAS. There was no time to lose. On learning of this new development, I contacted the Washington office for application materials and other information on the scholarship program. The office responded promptly and sent the application form as well as a brochure containing detailed information about the fellowship program.

For some reason, there was a lull in my enthusiasm to go to graduate school. So I tucked away the application form and other information from the OAS in my office desk drawer at the conference office and forgot all about the idea for the time being. From time to time, my wife would nudge me to pursue a graduate degree in public health. And even though I gave her reasons why I was not pushing ahead with this as vigorously as I had at an earlier time, she persisted that once the opportunity came my way I should not delay in embarking on my intended study program. Her constant encouragement propelled me in the direction of pursuing graduate studies in public health after all.

In late November 1996, while attending the Caribbean Union Conference's year-end meetings in Trinidad. I met with the new health ministries and ADRA director of the Caribbean Union Conference, Dr. Noel Brathwaite. As we exchanged plans and projections for the the work of Health Ministries and ADRA, both regionally and specifically in Guyana, he seemed very impressed with the progress of the work under my watch. During our discussion, he asked if I had any plans to pursue graduate study in the field of public health. I told him that I was giving that prospect some serious thought and at the same time exploring options in that regard. He encouraged me to make it a matter of priority to pursue graduate studies in public health in the near future.

When I returned home after the meetings, I reflected on my conversation with Dr. Braithwaite. I told my wife what had transpired, and she reinforced Dr. Braithwaite's advice. The more I thought about the prospect of actually pursuing graduate studies in public health, the more motivated I felt to take decisive steps to realize that dream.

A few days after my return to the office following my attendance at the year-end meetings in Trinidad, a thought crossed my mind. Since I was already in receipt of application materials from the OAS, I might as well go ahead and complete the application form and submit it for review. I decided to act upon this immediately and, therefore, reached into my drawer and retrieved the application package from the OAS. Before filling out the application form, I called the local OAS office for information on application deadlines for its fellowship program for the 1997-98 academic year.

I was pleasantly surprised to discover, when I contacted the local OAS office, that a few days ago that office had placed a notice in the national newspapers calling for applications for fellowship awards for the 1997-98 academic year. The closing date for the receipt of applications was Friday, December 6. That meant I had only one week to complete the application process and get all the required supporting documents turned in. God providentially had led me to contact the local OAS office at the time I did. I immediately got to work filling out the application.

One of the stipulations regarding the scholarship award was the applicant's prior acceptance into an accredited university. This was one instance in my life when preparation met opportunity. I contacted Loma Linda University and asked them to fax me a copy of my current letter of acceptance into the public health program there.

Within a day of making the request to Loma Linda, the university faxed me a copy of my letter. In less than a week, I had completed the application and submitted it to the local OAS office. The application was then forwarded to the Public Service Ministry Scholarship Division for processing. The Lord had guided me to this source of funding and helped me to meet the deadline at short notice. The smooth way in which the process was unfolding was evidence that God was leading.

Within a week of submission of the application, I received a call from the scholarship coordinator at the Public Service Ministry. "Good morning. This is the chief training officer in the Training and Scholarships Division of the

Public Service Ministry. Am I speaking with Alexander Isaacs?"

"Yes, this is Alexander Isaacs."

"Mr. Isaacs, I am calling in connection with your recent application for a government of Guyana award to study for the master of public health degree at Loma Linda University School of Public Health through the OAS."

Those words were like music to my ears.

"I would like you to come to our office for an interview on Wednesday at 1:00 p.m."

"Thank you for inviting me. I will be there at 1:00 p.m."

I could hardly believe my good fortunes. I reasoned that the fact that they had called me for an interview meant that there was a chance that I would receive the scholarship award. I prayed earnestly to God, asking Him to have His way in this matter. I felt very optimistic that my application would be considered favorably. I could hardly wait for Wednesday to roll around.

I prepared for the interview as best I could and saturated the waiting process with much prayer for God's guidance and will to be revealed.

Notwithstanding my optimism at the prospect of receiving the scholarship, a major hurdle loomed ahead. Since most of the scholarships issued by the Public Service Ministry were offered to individuals who worked in the government, I felt a certain degree of trepidation since I was not in active government service. This could well prove to be a mitigating factor in the award of a fellowship from that body. I, nonetheless, decided to attend the interview and leave the outcome in God's hands.

I showed up for the interview at the time appointed and was ushered into the coordinator's office. After exchanging greetings, the officer interviewed me for the fellowship award. Among other things, I was told that, because of the potential usefulness of my intended study program to Guyana's future development, she was willing to recommend me to the scholarship decision makers as a worthy and timely investment in such an award. The terms and conditions of the award were then laid out.

During the interview, I learned that the OAS fellowship award necessitated a contractual obligation with the Guyana government for a specified period of time on completion of one's study program. The officer then asked if I was willing to serve the Guyana government for a specified period of time on my return to Guyana at the end of my student program in the United States. I surmised that on return to Guyana after the completion of my study program I may be allowed to work for the Seventh-day Adventist Church in lieu of the government, especially since there was a clause in the contract that allowed for such an option. However, such an arrangement would first have to be approved by the government. It seemed a fair question although I did not know then how that would factor into my future plans on my return to Guyana. I gave verbal assent to that precondition, resolving in my mind that if the government allowed it I would fulfill my contractual obligation to the government while working for the Adventist Church. If the government did not approve of such an arrangement, I resolved to accept whatever job placement I was given. I consoled myself with the fact that such an assignment with the government would have a time limit attached to it anyway after which I would be free to return to full-time denominational employment.

In a nutshell, I reasoned that I had much to gain by accepting the scholarship offer from the OAS/government of Guyana and that the least I could do was to render whatever period of service the government would require in return for the scholarship award. This encounter encouraged me to be optimistic about the outcome of my application, notwithstanding the uncertainties that surfaced at that time.

Approximately six weeks after the interview, I was called to a second interview with the training coordinator. On arrival at PSM for that meeting I was ushered into the coordinator's office. The officer was in another part of the building. As I awaited the officer's return, I prayed for God's guidance and the outworking of His will. The officer eventually returned and greeted me with, "Alexander, I have called you to let you know that I have recommended you for the scholarship award from the Organization of American States. The government in turn has endorsed your application, which has since been forwarded to the OAS for consideration. You should be hearing from them on the outcome of your application by early June of this year. Let's keep our fingers crossed."

"Thank you very much. I really appreciate your efforts in this regard."

"Remember, Alexander, that should you be considered for a scholarship by the OAS, you will be required to serve the government on your return to Guyana at the end of your study program in the United States."

"I am aware of my obligation in that regard and stand ready to honor it."

She continued, "I will keep you posted on further developments in this regard."

"Thank you."

This was most welcomed news. I thanked God for granting me favor in the eyes of the governmental authorities, and I pleaded with Him to do the same with the OAS officials who handled the final processing of the scholarship application.

Apart from a few of my very close family members and the conference administration, the prospect of receiving a scholarship from the OAS to study in the United States was not shared with anyone else.

My wife was pleased with the way things were unfolding. And now, with the high likelihood of my receiving the scholarship award from the OAS to study in the United States of America, she was delighted.

Even though I did not have final confirmation of the scholarship award, I began putting things in place for my impending departure to the United States.

As June approached, I became very anxious. I had not heard anything further about the scholarship award. During the second week of June, I left Guyana to attend the Caribbean Union Conference of Seventh-day Adventists mid-year committee meetings in Trinidad. I was absorbed in the business of the meetings when a thought about the scholarship crossed my mind.

It occurred to me then that it was around that time of year that the OAS headquarters was expected to announce its decision about fellowship awards for the 1997-98 school year. I reasoned then that if the OAS Trinidad office had received notification of its awardees, the OAS Guyana office would, most likely, have also been similarly informed. I felt impressed to call the OAS Trinidad and Tobago office to see if they had received any communication from the OAS headquarters pertaining to fellowship awards for Trinidad and Tobago applicants.

When I called the OAS Trinidad office, a female voice was on the other side of the line.

"Hello, good morning, OAS. How can I help you?"

"Good morning. I applied for an OAS fellowship earlier this year and have called to find out if your office has received any official communication from the OAS Washington office about the Trinidad and Tobago awardees for the 1997-98 academic year."

"Yes, a few days ago, this office received a list of names of applicants from Trinidad and Tobago who have been awarded fellowships for the 1997-98 school year."

I could hardly believe my ears. Then she asked,

"What is your name?"

"Alexander Isaacs"

"Okay, please hold while I check the list to see if your name is there."

After a brief while she came back with, "I'm sorry, your name is not on our list of awardees. Are you from Trinidad and Tobago?"

"No. I am a Guyanese national. I somehow was of the opinion that Caribbean OAS fellowship awardees would be communicated in block rather than country by country."

"Unfortunately that is not the case. Each territory is communicated with

Thy Will Be Done

directly by OAS Washington."

"Do you know if the Guyana office was communicated with similarly?"

"No, I am not privy to such information but I would suggest that you call them to find out."

As soon as we broke for lunch I called the OAS Guyana Office. "Good morning," said the person who answered the phone.

"Good day. This is Pastor Alexander Isaacs."

"Pastor Isaacs! I was just about to call you at the conference office."

"Is that so?"

"Yes, we just received a fax from the OAS Washington office indicating that you have been awarded a fellowship to study at Loma Linda University for the 1997 fall semester. You will need to come to our office to finalize arrangements for your travel to the United States."

"Thank you, God," I blurted out over the telephone. "Thank you for sharing this information with me. I am currently attending a business meeting in Trinidad and will be returning home tonight. I will come in to the office in the morning."

As she hung up the telephone, I could hardly contain myself. Joy flooded my heart. This was like a dream come true. I would be able to study in the United States at the prestigious Loma Linda University School of Public Health with all expenses paid! What an overflowing blessing this was! I returned to the meeting, my heart filled with gratitude to God.

Although it was hard to keep the good news inside, I did not share it with anyone. For the rest of the meetings my thoughts were focused on my scholarship award and my impending departure to the United States.

I could not wait to inform my wife of this development until I returned home so I broke the news that evening via telephone after the meeting ended. She was elated. Her immediate words were, "God is good! Lead on, O King Eternal."

I returned to Guyana that same evening in the company of the other individuals who had attended the meetings.

The following day I visited the OAS Guyana office and met with the relevant personnel who updated me on the award and laid out the terms and conditions of the fellowship. I then contacted the training coordinator at the Public Service Ministry and expressed my thanks to her for her role in the process. I took that opportunity to start the necessary paper work associated with the fellowship award.

Chapter 19

Life at Loma Linda

After all of the paperwork was finalized, which took approximately two months, my family and I left Guyana for Loma Linda University to embark on my study program in public health. This was the moment I had looked forward to all along. Here was my opportunity to realize a lifelong dream.

While at Loma Linda University, I pursued a dual master's degree in public health with majors in international health and health promotion and education.

Our sojourn at Loma Linda University could be described as a nice blend of opportunities, challenges, and successes. It was a distinct privilege to be able to pursue my studies without having to worry about how my tuition fees and living expenses were going to be met. At the beginning of every quarter, when it was time for registration, I completed the process without any problems. The OAS took care of my tuition each quarter without fail. In addition to handling all my tuition expenses, they provided me with a monthly stipend for rent and living expenses.

Moreover, they fully funded my dual degree program in international health and health promotion and education as I had hoped for all along. However, this came with two main preconditions. Firstly, I had to maintain satisfactory academic progress measured by their standards, and secondly, I had to complete my study program within two years.

In order for me to complete my study program in the time frame stipulated, I attended classes year round, including summers. Coupled with this, I carried extra credits, sometimes as many as six credits above the average of eight per quarter. This was by no means easy, but God saw me through.

Unfortunately, the annual allocation by the OAS for books proved to be inadequate. In most instances, that sum was fully spent by the end of the first quarter of the school year. Therefore, I had to find additional money to cover the cost of books for the remainder of the school year. Added to this was the challenge of subsisting on the stipend provided by the OAS. After paying for rent, the remainder, even though handled frugally, was not sufficient to meet the combined needs of our family. The stipend from the OAS was meant to cover my personal expenses, including medical insurance, but it did not

Thy Will Be Done

provide coverage for any of my family expenses. When the high cost of health care was factored into our financial equation, it was clear that we needed another source of income to be able to survive. Since my wife was pregnant with our second son who was born there during my first year of studies, we needed insurance and additional savings for other maternity expenses.

Thankfully, through God's providential workings I was able to meet my expenses. By the second quarter of my study program, I became acquainted with Walter Harris, a permanent U.S. resident of Guyanese origin who resided in Loma Linda. He took it upon himself to seek out supplementary funding for my family from a variety of sources. Brother Harris provided me with regular part time work with his landscaping company. He also helped us furnish our apartment and connected us with a medical doctor by the name of John Gibson who contributed towards our monthly grocery needs in cash or kind.

He further introduced me to a retired nurse by the name of Elsie Wendth who adopted my family as her "missionary project." Whenever there was work to be done in her yard, she would call me to do it and pay me for it.

Brother Evans Lewis and family, overseas based Guyanese living in Loma Linda, invited us to lunch every Sabbath after church for the entire length of our stay at Loma Linda University. The only time we did not have Sabbath lunch at the Lewis' was when we chose not to show up for one reason or other. This family kept a constant eye out for my family's welfare. Each month, Brother Lewis also contributed to our upkeep in cash or kind.

Another family that was especially benevolent to my family during our sojourn at Loma Linda was Floyd and Beverly Martin, acquaintances I had met in Guyana in the late 70s. The Martins lived in Palmdale, which was approximately two and a half hours away from Loma Linda.

On learning that my family was at Loma Linda University, they made it their duty to assist in our welfare. This they did willingly and without any strings attached. We were invited to spend Thanksgiving with their family each year and at least one Christmas. At such gatherings we met with other acquaintances from Guyana and also made new friends.

I vividly recall a particular instance when God came through for us in a marvelous way.

It was a requirement of the university at that time that dependents possess adequate insurance coverage throughout their stay at Loma Linda. Such coverage could be provided through the department of Adventist Risk Management (ARM) on campus. However, such coverage came at a price. The student was required to pay the insurance premium for each dependent at the beginning of the quarter at the time of registration.

My wife was pregnant with our second son, and I therefore needed to provide coverage for the ensuing quarter for her, my elder son, and the unborn child. Without such coverage, my family would have no insurance for that entire quarter. Further, my wife would be unable to access the needed medical care during the course of her pregnancy because we were not in a position to pay for those expenses out of pocket.

At the time of registration, I could not make the payment for insurance premium. Notwithstanding this state of affairs, I had every intention to make good that payment before the term was through. I therefore asked ARM for a grace period to be able to make good my outstanding payment to that body. My request was granted.

As the term wore on and the due date for the birth of our second son drew closer, I was given constant reminders to pay my dependents' insurance premium or risk having my wife and the unborn suffer the consequences of being without adequate insurance coverage for the remainder of my wife's pregnancy as well as after delivery.

I made this an item of special prayer that God would provide the funding for me to be able to pay my family insurance. I explored a number of avenues in an effort to secure the required funding but without any success. The extended deadline for payment of the insurance premium would be up in a couple of days and still no breakthrough.

One Friday morning, three days before the expiration of the extended deadline date for the payment of my family's insurance premium to ARM, we pleaded with God during our morning devotions, to lead us to a source from which we could get the assistance. After worship, I felt impressed to call the university church's Adventist Community Services (ACS) office and request some financial assistance to be able to pay my family's insurance premium for that quarter. I was willing to accept whatever amount they were willing to contribute.

When I called the ACS office, the individual who answered the telephone asked me to drop by the office to discuss my request in more detail.

On my way to classes later that morning, I made a detour to the ACS Office as requested. I laid out my case to the person in charge and she promised to see how best they could assist. I was told to return on Monday morning at 9:00 a.m. by which time they hoped to receive some funds to be able to provide the requested assistance.

On Monday morning, I arrived at the ACS office in time for my 9:00 a.m. appointment. Up to that point the office had not received the promised income from the donor. After making a few follow up calls the supervisor said to me

Thy Will Be Done

that the expected funds did not come in so they were unable to be of assistance at that point in time. She apologized for not being able to assist and prayed with me for success in my attempts to raise the money. She made a passing remark that if funding was received subsequently she would get in touch with me. I thanked her for her willingness to help, and then left the office.

That morning, while in class, I could not concentrate on my studies. My mind was preoccupied with how I will fare if I did not get the required funding by the end of the day to be able to meet the ARM deadline.

At around 10:30 a.m. while hurrying along the main corridor of the School of Public Health on my way to my next class, one of my friends, Yohan, stopped me and said,

"Alexander, a few minutes ago, while walking by the public pay phone, I heard it ringing and decided to pick up the receiver. The person on the other side of the line identified herself as Mrs Isaacs and said that she was desperately trying to get in touch with you. She asked me if I knew you and when I said I did, she pleaded with me to get a message to you that you needed to call home immediately because she had a very important message for you. I was searching for you everywhere since then but could not locate you to give you the message. I think that you should call her right away."

"Thanks Yohan, I will call her immediately."

I called home using the same pay phone over which my friend had received the message earlier.

"Hello honey, one of my friends just told me that you were trying to reach me."

"Yes, my dear, I was trying to reach you over the telephone about an hour ago.

A lady called here around nine thirty this morning and said that she was from ACS. She asked that you check with them immediately concerning your request."

"Okay, I will do so right away."

"Yes, please do. She said that it was urgent."

I hung up the telephone and hurried off to the ACS office a few blocks away. I apologized for showing up one hour after they had called and explained that I had received the message only a couple of minutes ago.

"Alexander, I am glad you are here. This morning, just as you left our office, one of our donors walked through the door and donated US$500.00, the exact amount which you need to pay your family's insurance coverage with Adventist Risk Management by today's deadline. This has to be the hand of God at work for you!"

"Praise God!" I exclaimed.

"Here!" Enclosed in this envelope is a check for US$500.00 payable to Risk Management. Take it over to the Director right away and make your insurance premium payment."

I was overjoyed! As I held the envelope in my hand I thanked her profusely for this gesture. With no time to spare, I went straight to ARM and made the payment. I was dumbfounded at God's divine intervention in my life's affairs and for coming through for me just in the nick of time!

Not long after that incident, my second son was born at the Loma Linda Medical Center. With insurance coverage for both mother and child, they were able to receive the best medical care available in Loma Linda and its environs.

In the summer of 1998, my Integrated Community Development class from the School of Public Health visited Kenya and Tanzania. That trip was one of the most memorable experiences in my entire life. In addition to the learning experience gained, some of my favorite memories from the trip include a visit to France during the World Cup soccer finals between France and Brazil; the safari experience in Kenya; the warmth and cordiality of the African people; the feeling of delight in being able to visit part of "Mother Africa" during my lifetime; the opportunity to view the snowcapped peaks of Mount Kilimanjaro and ascend approximately 1,000 feet of that famous mountain in Tanzania; the trauma experienced during the bombing of the U.S. Embassy in Nairobi on the day we were returning to the United States; and being able to observe firsthand the rich African culture. All of these experiences have left indelible impressions on my mind. I am nostalgic whenever I remember our trip to Africa. If afforded the opportunity to visit Africa again, I would be delighted to do so.

Just prior to departing for Africa, the Lord opened a way for me to secure a part-time job on campus as a research assistant in the Evaluation and Research Unit. On my return to Loma Linda after the Kenya and Tanzania trips, I began my job at the university. This additional source of income was most welcomed and helped to defray expenses not covered by the OAS award nor other supplementary sources of funding

With hard work and the blessings of God, I successfully completed my study at Loma Linda University and graduated in 1999. I remained on campus for a little under a year during which time I completed the culminating activities for my two majors. After I was through with those assignments, I was awarded my master's in public health degree. Around that same time, I received the Certified Health Education Specialist (CHES) credential from the National Commission for Health Education Counseling, Inc., after passing the prescribed examinations. On completing my studies, I ignored all the

Thy Will Be Done

allurements of remaining in the United States and, in keeping with my pledge to the government of Guyana, my family and I returned to our home land at the end of May 2000.

Chapter 20

Government Service

I held out high hopes that on my return to Guyana, the government would allow me to work in the Health Ministries Department of the Guyana Conference of Seventh-day Adventists. I wanted to work for the church again and be discharged from my contractual obligations to the government.

My optimism in this regard was fueled by a particular clause in my contract that stipulated that on returning to Guyana after completion of my training program, I had the option of accepting a job with a non-governmental organization involved in substantial health care delivery. Of course, as mentioned earlier, such an agreement had to be approved by the government.

The work carried out by the Health Ministries Department of the Adventist Church in Guyana is national in scope. Therefore, I sought the approval of the government to be placed with the conference for the duration of my contract. At that time, the church had vacancies for a health ministries director and a country director for ADRA. The conference administration was more than willing to have me rejoin the staff on a full-time basis.

I waited with eager anticipation for the government's endorsement of my request. The prospects of getting the go-ahead seemed quite good.

I had many ideas on how I would move the work of health ministries and ADRA forward. But to my dismay, my request to the government was denied on the grounds that, in their view, the Adventist Church's Health Ministries Department did not qualify as an alternative health agency for the placement of a government of Guyana scholarship recipient. This being so, I had to forego, at least for the time being, some of the ambitious plans I had. This meant that I would have to accept whatever job placement the government offered.

Because of the nature of my graduate training, I had the premonition that I would be placed in the public health sector. Even though I had worked in the public sector before, I had not worked in the health sector. Therefore, I did not know what to expect. At the time of signing my contract with the government, I had agreed to accept whatever job placement I was given on the completion of my studies. If this was the way the Lord would have it, I concluded, then I would follow His will. The contract was for three years after which time I would be free to return to full-time denominational employment if I chose to.

After being interviewed by a number of departments within the public health sector, the government granted me employment with the Social Impact Amelioration Project (SIMAP) as coordinator of health services. SIMAP was established in the late 1980s to cushion the impact of the Guyana Government's Economic Recovery Program (ERP) on the poorer segments of the population. I accepted my job assignment quite willingly and resolved to give it my best shot.

At SIMAP I was responsible for the management of the health and nutrition sub-projects, which were being funded by the Inter-American Development Bank (IDB). Because of the varied nature and scope of the work undertaken by the department where I was assigned, I received exposure to a wide variety of work situations. The breadth and depth of learning acquired during my graduate training at Loma Linda University served to facilitate my work in remarkable ways by affording me a great degree of versatility and competence in the field of public health. Moreover, my work met with the approval of my employers more than I could imagine.

I felt a real sense of satisfaction in being able to effect the turnaround of SIMAP's Health Department and restore its credibility, which had been severely eroded over the years. Staff morale, which was at an all-time low when I joined the department, was boosted, and everyone had a more optimistic outlook of the future of the department.

Also, during my tenure at SIMAP, my department was instrumental in developing and implementing a national Good Young-Child Feeding Program. That program has since become the standard for young-child feeding in the whole nation. Owing to the program's high quality, it placed third in the Caribbean Food and Nutrition Institute's (CFNI) Caribbean-wide 2002 annual awards for outstanding work in health and nutrition.

In 2002 I was transferred to the Health Sector Development Unit (HSDU) of the Ministry of Health as technical assistant to the project coordinator.

My principal assignment at the HSDU was to play a lead role in the design, planning, development, and implementation of the Basic Nutrition Program.

The Basic Nutrition Program was a bold initiative by the government to reduce malnutrition among women and young children in poor communities in the country. It also sought to strengthen the implementation capacity of the public sector. Our goal was to improve the nutritional status of high-risk groups and reduce malnutrition-related illnesses and deaths related to poverty. The project proposal was approved and the government received funding for the program through the Inter-American Development Bank. This program

Government Service

met with tremendous success and has since become entrenched into the national public health system.

Some of my other assignments while working with the HSDU included helping with the coordination and distribution of national resources according to need, helping to improve quality and range of services available to the disadvantaged, and ensuring that existing health resources were used more efficiently. I was also responsible for improving the performance of the civil service through administrative reforms, helping to establish self-governing hospitals and Regional Health Authorities, and improving the functioning of the Ministry of Health. In addition, I assisted in the design of a major HIV/AIDS Prevention and Control Program. Further, toward the end of 2002, I had the honor of representing the government at a special Caribbean Area Public Health course which was held in Japan.

Additionally, I was afforded the privilege of interacting with a number of national and international donors including the Inter-American Development Bank, the World Bank, and the United Nations Family Planning Association (UNFPA). Two results of such interactions were the enhanced learning and firsthand knowledge of how those international financial institutions operated. I was also able to forge important business relationships with the public and private health sectors and international NGOs.

With regards to my contribution to the advancement of the work of the church during this period of employment with the government, I was able to serve as health ministries director, ADRA Guyana country director, and pastor all in a part-time capacity. This afforded me the unique opportunity of serving both church and state simultaneously. Even though this placed heavy demands on my time, I enjoyed it and felt privileged to be able to serve in these capacities.

During the 2001-02 academic year, the University of Guyana engaged my services as a part-time lecturer in the department of health sciences. I taught nutrition to the final year students in the nursing program and second year students in the medical program. I immensely enjoyed my teaching stint at the University of Guyana.

Rather than being an impediment, my work assignment in the public health sector turned out to be a very exciting, enriching, and rewarding experience. I believe that God strategically placed me in those work environments so that, as I served the nation in varied capacities, I would be able to acquire skills and experience that would prove invaluable in my future work with the church. God was indeed guiding, leading, and preparing me all along for wider service.

Chapter 21

Employment Decisions

Working part-time for the church while simultaneously fulfilling my contract with the government kept me in touch with pastoral ministry. Throughout my tenure with the government, I pastored a church in the city. Thus, in effect, I was still able to carry out ministerial functions, though on a scaled-down basis, while doing the statewide planning for health reform that would enable thousands of people to live healthier lives.

I enjoyed working with the government. My training and expertise were being put to use at the national level. I was serving the needs of a wide cross-section of the Guyanese population. My job was rewarding and brought me a great deal of personal satisfaction. In addition, the pay was good, offering a sure opportunity to provide a better economic future for my family.

By the time I had only one year left on my contract with the government, I had become so caught up in my work with the state that the prospect of returning to full-time denominational employment, at least in the immediate future, was a remote consideration. As a matter of fact, as my contract neared its end, many lucrative options for future employment with the government were placed before me.

Firstly, the Ministry of Health asked that I continue to serve as technical coordinator until the Basic Nutrition Program was formally implemented. Once the program was up and running, I was earmarked to serve as its program manager. Secondly, the Ministry of Health made me a lucrative offer to serve as the chief executive officer of Regional Health Authorities in two administrative regions in the country. Thirdly, on account of my successful stint of teaching at the University of Guyana, that institution made me an offer to join the faculty of health sciences in the School of Medicine as a full-time lecturer.

Another lucrative job prospect before me was to serve as health education officer with the Pan American Health Organization/World Health Organization (PAHO/WHO) office in Guyana.

Several other attractive job prospects within the public and private sectors beckoned me.

In actual fact, these non-denominational prospects of employment were

Employment Decisions

to be desired. They carried with them attractive remuneration packages when compared with full-time denominational employment. If I chose the former, the natural inclination would be to remain employed by the government so that I could provide a better financial future for my family.

As the end of my contract with the government drew nearer, the realization that I would need to make a definite choice in regards to my future employment struck me forcibly. Either I pursued a full-time career with the government or I returned to full-time denominational employment. This was by no means a straightforward decision. As with the rest of my life decisions, I sought God's guidance and will for my life.

To find out His will, I thought long and hard on this matter and engaged in much prayer and fasting. It soon became apparent that I would have to employ a variety of approaches since no one approach would be sufficient in helping me to make the right choice.

First, I made this decision a matter of daily prayer. During my daily personal and family devotions, as well as throughout the day, I sent up my petitions to God and asked Him for His guidance as I worked through this situation.

Next, I sought the advice of others I trusted. In doing so, I got mixed reactions. Some individuals suggested that I continued to work with the government full time and work for the church on a part-time basis. Others advised that even though the salary of a denominational worker with my qualifications and experience was not as lucrative as that offered by the government, I should return to full-time denominational employment, with the full assurance that as I did so God will continue to provide for the needs of my family. Such diametrically opposed views made it even more difficult for me to make a choice between the two options before me.

I considered the pros and cons of both career options, carefully examining the subject under consideration. The detailed nature of this approach gave me the opportunity to work through the situation in a systematic manner. As I did so, several things jumped out at me. Firstly, my services were equally in demand by the government as well as by the church. As a matter of fact, as far as I knew, there was no one else in the country with my kind of specialized training. Secondly, as mentioned earlier, the government's remuneration package was much more lucrative than that which I hoped to receive from employment with the church. Thirdly, leaving the Ministry of Health at that time would pose some serious challenges as regards to finding a suitable replacement for my position. After all, I was the one earmarked to supervise the national Basic Nutrition Program, the implementation of which was about to commence. Since I had played a major role in the program's design, I had a good understanding of how it would evolve once it got underway, Therefore, for all practical purposes, I was regarded as the most suitable person to lead out in the project's implementation.

As I continued to analyze the pros and cons, I reasoned that the prospects for upward mobility within the National Health System were quite good. Moreover, remaining in government employment would provide me with a unique opportunity to do good for many people on a much larger scale than the personal one of my role as a minister and supplicant.

However, deciding to continue working for the government would mean that I would have to forgo the prospects of ordination since, at that time, as a general rule, the church would not ordain me unless I was a full-time denominational worker.

Alternatively, there were several pros to returning to full-time denominational employment. Whereas the public health sector had at its disposal a number of health practitioners with advanced degrees in a variety of health disciplines, there was a severe shortage of skilled, qualified public health and development personnel within the church to perform the management functions associated with the running of the health ministries and ADRA departments at the Guyana Conference of SDA. Based on such prevailing conditions in the church scenario, it became quite clear to me that in order for the work of the health ministries and ADRA departments to move forward, there was an urgent need for well-qualified personnel in the work force at the conference level.

All things equal, I believed that someone with my kind of training and professional experience in public health would be an invaluable asset to the church especially in these two departments. Further, as mentioned before, my choice of majors for my graduate studies in public health was influenced to a large extent by the need for workers with such expertise within the church organization. At the time of my choice of these two majors, my hope was to be able to manage the health ministries and ADRA departments simultaneously once my training program was completed and if there was a need for my services within the organization at that time. Even though there were no ADRA projects up and running in the conference at that time, there were a number of funding sources both nationally and internationally, through which the agency could access funding.

After considering all these options, there was no doubt in my mind that should I return to full-time denominational employment at that time I would be instrumental in generating project ideas and locating funding for same. Besides, the regional and divisional ADRA offices in Trinidad and Miami, respectively, were amenable to supporting ADRA initiatives in Guyana.

Employment Decisions

Having worked with the church in both capacities on a full-time basis previously and on a part-time basis in recent years, I had no doubt that I would enjoy a great deal of job satisfaction in my dual roles as full-time health ministries director and ADRA Guyana country director. Besides, due to the nature and extent of my work in these two departments of the church, the services rendered would also have a national impact, even though not on the same level as if I were to remain working for the government. Another factor favoring my return to full-time denominational employment was the fact that I would get ample opportunity for continuing education and on-the-job training.

A very significant aspect of the process of making a choice in this matter was my wife's whole-hearted endorsement of the prospects of taking up full-time denominational employment once more. She felt strongly, as I did, that the Lord was leading me in this direction.

Also, an assessment of the work climate within the church at that time, especially as it related to ADRA, suggested that it was an opportune time for me to get back into full-time denominational work. From all appearances, doing so would augur well for my future advancement and upward mobility within the organization.

My emotions varied throughout the entire decision-making process. While still in the "valley of decision," I reflected on a testimony shared by the editor of the *Adventist Review*, Pastor William G. Johnsson, in his 1990 devotional *Behold His Glory*. In one of his readings titled "The Call," on pages 67 and 68, Pastor Johnsson shared two inspirational stories, one from the life of Jesus and one from his own.

In that particular devotional reading, Pastor Johnsson quoted a passage from *The Desire of Ages* by Ellen G. White about Jesus' recognition and response to the call.

"Tidings of the wilderness prophet [John the Baptist] … spread throughout Galilee.… In Nazareth it was told in the carpenter's shop that had been Joseph's, and One recognized the call. His time had come. Turning from His daily toil, He bade farewell to His mother, and followed in the steps of His countrymen who were flocking to the Jordan."

Johnsson then asked a rhetorical question: "How did Jesus know it, know that His time had come?" Johnsson went on to write the following in response to the question posed.

"He was then about 30 (Luke 3:23)—certainly no age for impetuous action. Nazareth may have been provincial, but it was safe. Nazareth stood for home and security. But when Jesus closed the door on the carpenter's shop, He chose the unknown. He opted for the open road instead of security, for unpredictable

Thy Will Be Done

happenings, and misunderstandings and abuse. And at last—for a cross.

God calls, No one can explain it: *how, when, or why*. There are false calls—God doesn't call everyone who *feels* called; but God calls. And when God calls, the heart must respond. It must weigh Nazareth against Calvary" (emphasis mine).

Turning attention to his own experience, Johnsson noted that for three years he had worked as an industrial chemist. Having earned a bachelor's degree in technology by the age of 19, he went to work in the industry in research and development. He portrayed the following scenario which was similar to my current situation.

"I had friends; the salary was good; the job offered security, and prospects for promotion. But one day I left it all behind. For some months, I'd been wrestling with a sense of God's calling, trying to argue God and myself out of it. At last I yielded to the divine imperative. I wrote a letter of resignation and left it on the desk of the chief chemist. He was amazed, shocked. He thought at first that I had been bought out by a rival company in the same city. When I told him that I was quitting chemistry, despite my love for it, for the uncertain prospect of ministry, he stared at me uncomprehending."

Johnsson concluded the reading with these words. "God calls. That was the hardest decision of my life.... So Jesus shut up the shop, said good-bye to Mary, and set out for the Jordan. I'm glad He did. His sense of mission gives me my place in the world."

I was impressed by the two testimonies shared by Johnsson. Jesus' resoluteness and Johnsson's yielding to the claims of God on his life by walking away from a lucrative career to take up full-time ministry caught my attention and personally spoke to me.

When I summed up the pros and cons of returning to full-time denominational employment at that point and time, I knew full well that such a move would entail a lot of faith and sacrifice. It would also cost my family opportunities. Many of the privileges they currently enjoyed would have to be sacrificed. My children would be denied some of the comforts in life that they had grown accustomed to during my tenure with the government.

After several months of thorough consideration of the matter at hand, I had to make my choice. My future lay in the balance. I could remain in the "valley of decision" no longer. It was time for me to choose a way forward.

In the end I felt an irresistible urge to return to full-time denominational employment instead of continuing to work for the government. I became convinced that it was time for me to fully get on board with the work of the Lord once more. Like Johnsson and Jesus, and no doubt countless others, I made a conscious decision to return to full-time work with the church in spite of the inherent challenges that that decision would bring. God had guided me in making such a decision, and I was determined to follow Him no matter the consequences.

Soon after making my decision to return to full-time denominational employment, I wrote a letter of resignation and submitted it to my immediate supervisor at the Health Sector Development Unit. He was unpleasantly surprised. My decision did not meet with his approval. As a matter of fact, he gave me a number of reasons why I should not leave the Ministry of Health at that point and time. With some persuasion from several officials within the Ministry of Health, and taking into consideration the needs of the Basic Nutrition Program, which was in its final stages of readiness for implementation, I decided to extend my stay with the Ministry of Health for an additional six months. During that period of time, I worked diligently to establish all the mechanisms necessary for a smooth implementation of the Basic Nutrition Project. I even assisted in the process of trying to find and train a suitable replacement before leaving my position.

During this extended period with the Ministry of Health, I had time to reflect on my decision to return to full-time denominational employment. The more I thought about it, the more convinced I became that I had made the right decision in the prevailing circumstances. I resolved to stick to my decision. Somehow, I felt like Moses who chose to cast in his lot with the people of God and forsake the pleasures of Egypt at a time when the children of Israel needed him most. Fortunately, my wife supported me fully in my decision, and I returned to full-time denominational work in January 2004.

Chapter 22

Serving the Lord Through Ministry

Upon officially resigning from working for the government, I was reappointed health ministries director and ADRA Guyana country director with the Guyana Conference on a full-time basis. I immediately began expanding the work of ADRA and health ministries in the conference.

At that time, little was known about ADRA's operations in Guyana. Active programs were virtually nonexistent. A major constraint was the unavailability of money for operations and project funding.

Working in tandem with the administration of the Guyana Conference of Seventh-day Adventists, the cause of ADRA was championed in various quarters throughout the organizational structure of the church. The conference administration invested financial resources into ADRA's operations and supported my efforts to get the agency up and running once more.

I reconstituted the ADRA Guyana board of directors, exercising great care to ensure that the board members were drawn from a variety of professional backgrounds with many years of experience in their line of work.

In an effort to generate new project ideas, I sent out a request for project proposals. The response was overwhelming. Within a month, more than forty proposals covering the spectrum of ADRA's five portfolios, namely basic education, economic development, primary health, food security, and disaster preparedness and response were received. The project costs ranged between G$60,000 to G$40,000,000.

A concerted effort was made to locate money for the requested projects. Between 2004 and 2009 funds amounting to more than US$200,000 were received from a variety of sources, including the ADRA *Most Useful Gift Catalog*, ADRA/Canada, ADRA/UK, the Ministry of Health/World Bank, Ingathering Hope for Humanity, the Guyana Conference of Seventh-day Adventists, the Caribbean Union Conference, the Inter-American Division, and ADRA International. The monies received were used to fund several of the projects that had been submitted.

Serving the Lord Through Ministry

The work of ADRA in Guyana was accentuated during the 2005 floods that hit the country hard. Working in collaboration with the Guyana Conference of Seventh-day Adventists, ADRA was able to secure one 40-foot container of relief supplies and $25,000 U.S. dollars. These were all utilized in disaster response efforts. The work of ADRA was recognized and appreciated by the beneficiaries and the government. Local newspapers and television stations covered ADRA Guyana's and the Seventh-day Adventist Church's relief efforts. Furthermore, the SDA Church was singled out for special mention at several forums as having provided timely assistance during the disaster.

In 2007 ADRA Guyana received a 40-foot container of shoeboxes from ADRA/UK for distribution to orphans and vulnerable children in Guyana. Each year, ADRA/UK chooses a developing country as a beneficiary of a special Shoebox Appeal program. Through this program, individuals in the UK and overseas donate new items to needy children. The items are placed in shoeboxes and then shipped to the beneficiary country for distribution. Guyana was singled out for such assistance for the 2008 Shoebox Appeal program. The items in the shoeboxes included school supplies and personal effects. Shoeboxes were distributed to beneficiaries at more than twenty-six orphanages and children's homes run by the Ministry of Human Services and Social Security. In addition, shoeboxes were given to children in needy areas in the community and school children from schools recommended by the Ministry of Education as being in need of such assistance.

To keep my knowledge current in the area of ADRA related work and development, I attended a number of the training programs put on by the ADRA Professional Leadership Institute (APLI). I also served as a member of the ADRA International Policy Steering Committee for two years where I had the opportunity to contribute to the formulation of policies for the ADRA Network.

One of ADRA's many contributions to nation building was the donation of a large quantity of worm medication, which was in scarce supply, to the Ministry of Health for use in its nationwide worm infestation reduction campaign.

Collaborations were forged with government ministries, a number of national and international non-governmental organizations, and diplomatic missions, among others. This was very encouraging.

In the execution of my duties as ADRA country director, I had ample opportunity to bring to bear the knowledge and experience acquired during my years of working for the government. That proved to be invaluable. Additionally, the relationships forged during my years of service in the public sector proved to be advantageous in moving the work of ADRA forward. My academic and professional expertise were augmented by attendance at several ADRA-sponsored meetings and workshops, which was crucial to my understanding of the organization's operations.

In the Health Ministries Department, a variety of health initiatives got underway. In an effort to make health resources available to the constituency, the health ministries director of the General Conference of Seventh-day Adventists Inter-American Division, Dr. Elie Honore, was invited to facilitate a weekend seminar for church health secretaries and other health professionals. The aim of the workshop was to help participants plan for and conduct activities within their respective churches as well as share ideas on how to impact their communities in a meaningful way through health ministry. Dr Honore emphasized innovative approaches to health ministry and sought to revive initiatives that foster this "right arm" of the Gospel. At the end of the workshop, participants were unanimous in their appreciation for the rich experience gained.

In order to strengthen and expand the health work, several collaborative efforts were fostered with the Davis Memorial Hospital (DMH), the Seventh-day Adventist mission hospital in Guyana. One of the major collaborative ventures with DMH was the implementation of the Foundation Health Care (FHC) Workers Course in 2001.

I first learned of the initiative while a student at Loma Linda University. Just around that time, Dr. Richard Hart, who was dean of the School of Public Health, had founded Adventist Health International (AHI) with the sole purpose of strengthening mission hospitals that were struggling so that they could function more efficiently. DMH was one of the first three hospitals that AHI decided to assist in that regard.

Dr. Hart sought to groom me to play a meaningful role at DMH on my return to Guyana after the completion of my study program at Loma Linda University. It was during that period that proposals were written and funding received for the FHC program.

Many of the young people in Guyana have no job skills when they finish high school, and they have no opportunity for further education. This nine-month practical training course in health care skills was intended to give these young people employment opportunities as well as provide a springboard for entrance into advanced training programs. The Ministry of Health and the Institute of Distance and Continuing Education (IDCE) at the University of Guyana endorsed the program. The Ministry of Health agreed to award official certificates, jointly with DMH, to students who successfully completed the training program. The IDCE also agreed to award official certificates to successful program participants. Further, we established an agreement with the University of Guyana to accept the program as partial fulfillment of the entry requirements for the university's technician level courses in X-ray, medical technology, and pharmacy.

Through the FHC program, a number of young people have been trained and the majority of graduates have received gainful employment in the health care industry. Others have gone on to receive further training as medical doctors, registered nurses, nursing assistants, radiologists, lab technicians, and pharmacists, as well as pursue other lines of work in the healthcare field.

The FHC course has since received full registration with the National Accreditation Council of Guyana. Steps are currently underway to upgrade the course to the level where it can be used as one of the options for admission into the General Nursing Council of Guyana Nursing Assistant program.

Another major collaborative venture with DMH was the staging, in April 2004, of a special golden anniversary celebration of the Adventist health work in Guyana. Highlights of this event were a fitness walk; health lectures in schools; health screening booths at locations across the city, which offered free diabetes screening; special church services; and a health exhibition on the lawns of the hospital.

Then there was the coordination of the annual Overseas Medical Assistance Team (OMAT) visits and outreach activities in Guyana. This Guyanese-U.S. based group of health professionals visited Guyana yearly. During their visits, surgical procedures were carried out at significantly reduced rates, clinics were held in Georgetown and Linden, free self-breast examinations were offered at strategic locations, and first aid certificate training was conducted at DMH.

Another collaborative activity with DMH was the implementation of the Community Health Educators' Program (CHE). This program was started in an attempt to respond to the adverse effects that diabetes and hypertension were having on the Guyanese population. To jump start this program, a cadre of volunteer community workers, mostly women, from the SDA churches and other faith-based groups received training in diabetes education, screening skills for diabetes and hypertension, nutrition, weight management, and exercise. The first batch of trainees graduated on April 1, 2007. Upon graduating from the training program, the community health educators were sent back to their respective churches and communities to offer diabetes education and screening services on a voluntary basis.

Then there was the DMH Ready Care Program, a collaborative effort between the Ministry of Health, Davis Memorial Hospital, Catholic Relief Services, and the Health Ministries Department of the conference. This program catered for persons living with HIV/AIDS as well as those who were at risk of contracting the disease. The services offered were free of charge.

Thy Will Be Done

Additionally, through this program a cross-section of the SDA Church membership received training in voluntary counseling and testing services, and testing sites were set up at selected churches so that community residents could have access to these much-needed services in their respective communities.

Collaborative ventures were also undertaken with government, non-profit organizations, and faith-based organizations in an effort to train individuals in how to address the HIV/AIDS pandemic in Guyana. As part of efforts to deal with AIDS, the last Saturday of November was designated AIDS Awareness Day by the SDA Church. This provides a unique opportunity for the Adventist Church to make a significant input in the fight with HIV/AIDS. The Health Ministries Department sends materials to the churches to use in educating the community and the church membership on how to show compassion for those affected by HIV/AIDS.

In the summer of 2005, ADRA and the health ministries departments partnered with Loma Linda University's School of Public Health to host the Integrated Community Development class in Guyana. This was a special learning experience, and it provided me with the unique opportunity of sharing in the facilitation of the class's activities and engaging in the exchange of information with faculty, students, the public and private sectors, and community groups at various levels of the development spectrum. It was a real pleasure collaborating with my alma mater in the planning and execution of this initiative.

In an effort to equip the SDA clergy with theoretical and hands-on HIV/AIDS counseling skills, workshops were held from time to time. Conference administrators, departmental directors, and pastors received specialized training in HIV counseling techniques. Those who participated in the workshops attested to the high quality of specialized training received, as well as the relevance of such training in the varied lines of their work. The clergy were thus better equipped to relate more intelligently to their members, as well as those in their community suffering from HIV/AIDS.

By the grace of God and the support of the constituency, the Health Ministries Department had become vibrant once more and was making an indelible impression on the lives of many.

Chapter 23

Pastoral Responsibilities

In addition to my work with ADRA and the Health Ministries Department, I remained integrally involved in church administration and evangelism. Since completing theological training in 1992 and taking up employment with the Guyana Conference of Seventh-day Adventists, I have always been actively involved in pastoral ministry in one form or another in conjunction with my other managerial responsibilities at the conference level.

Shortly after my return to Guyana from the United States in 2000, I was assigned as the pastor of the Moriah Seventh-day Adventist Church in the Georgetown #2 District. It was as if I had picked up from where I had left off before departing for the U.S. in 1997.

In keeping with the evangelistic thrust of the church, I conducted evangelistic crusades at intervals throughout my ministry. Most of these were held at various locations in the city. On some occasions the circumstances were daunting, but with God's help and that of the membership, I fearlessly proclaimed the Word of God night after night. It was a real joy to see hundreds attending the meetings to hear Bible truths.

In 2001 I participated in what I consider as one of the most fulfilling, rewarding, and meaningful experiences in my pastoral ministry when I served as the "reader" and appeal singer for one of the largest evangelistic campaigns ever to be held in Guyana. Pastor Roosevelt Daniels, Caribbean Union evangelist, was the speaker. Each night, for eight weeks, I worked in tandem with the evangelist by reading specified passages of Scripture which he announced. As the series continued, and I went about my daily chores, I was referred to fondly as "reader" by children as well as adults. On a number of occasions, I saw little children pointing me out to their parents with words like, "Mummy, look. He's the reader at Pastor Daniels' crusade."

I was at a spiritual high during those meetings where I experienced first hand the dynamics of soul winning. After each nightly presentation, the evangelist assembled the pastors and Bible workers who showed an interest in learning further about soul winning and went over the night's sermon with us. During those sessions he took care to focus on the high points of the sermon as

Thy Will Be Done

well as go over specific evangelistic techniques used. This was a most enriching experience, and I walked away from each session better equipped to advance the kingdom of God through evangelism.

The crusade impacted and blessed many. At the conclusion of the meetings, more than eleven hundred new converts had been won to Christ. I was specially assigned to pastor the new flock.

The Conference administration had designated the Olivet SDA Church to house the new converts. However, as the crusade neared its end, the building was far from ready.

For a number of years the Olivet Church had languished in an old wooden structure, which was infested with termites and rodents. Burglars plagued the wooden structures, and the building began to sink. The spiritual well-being of the membership suffered and the attendance at regular church services dwindled over time. In 1988, the church made a decision to replace the wooden building with a concrete structure.

Because of major financial challenges, the building project did not begin until six years later. The foundations had been laid and all the columns erected. In the ensuing years leading up to 2001, work was done sporadically.

Early in 2001, Pastor Philip Bowman, the conference president, assumed responsibility as the interim pastor of the congregation. Pastor Bowman stepped up the pace of the building project.

The strategy adopted for the completion of the church building included, among other things, the setting up of a district building committee that was responsible for advising, executing, and supervising major aspects of the building project; urging sacrificial giving by the church members; coordinating volunteer work from the membership; and seeking support from sister churches.

The conference administration injected a significant amount of funds into the building project. Additional funds were also received from other sources. Gifts in cash and building materials streamed in. When funds appeared to be running out, the Lord poured into the treasury the funds needed to keep the project moving forward. The churches within the district pooled their efforts and made monetary contributions to the building program. God performed miracle after miracle to ensure that the work kept apace.

By the time the crusade was over, the entire floor area had been sand-filled and cast in cement, the lighting was installed, some new pews had been built, a new sound system and other accessories were acquired. On November 2, 2001, the new converts, along with the existing members of the Olivet SDA Church, began worshiping in their new church building under my pastoral leadership.

A number of things still needed to be done on the building before it would be ready for dedication, so work continued at an accelerated pace.

As the church building project neared completion, one of the major constraints faced was the painting of the building. The estimated cost of the paint was somewhere in the vicinity of one million Guyanese dollars. When labor costs were factored in, another half a million dollars would be needed. The church was not in a position to fund this from its limited financial resources. We, therefore, prayed to God about the matter.

A member from one of our sister churches heard about our need for paint. He had an acquaintance with the manager of a prominent contracting firm in Georgetown. The church member raised the subject of painting the building with the contractor who in turn asked us to provide him with an estimate of the quantity of paint that was needed to complete the entire building. Once that was done he pledged to do what he could.

Within a week of submitting the estimate to the contractor, he provided all the painting materials needed to paint the interior and exterior of the building. This magnanimous gesture was received with jubilation and thankfulness. The painting job was completed a short time later.

At another critical point in the building project, funds were once again running low when the Lord impressed a member from one of our sister churches in the city to contribute nearly half a million dollars to the campaign. This donation took care of the immediate financial needs and served to keep the work moving forward. And so it was throughout the building program. The Lord performed one miracle after another. Every time funds ran low, God provided by either impressing the members to give sacrificially, providing funds through contacts outside the church, supplying in-kind assistance, or working through a combination of these three.

After a little less than two years of prayer, hard work, sacrifice, and God's miraculous provisions, the church was ready to be dedicated to the Lord. The ceremony took place on Sunday March 16, 2003. The occasion was one of pomp and circumstance as the church celebrated the achievement of a significant milestone. The members thanked God for His great provision. Indeed, the Lord had done great things whereof we were made glad.

All through my ministry, I looked forward to the day when I would be ordained to the Gospel ministry. Even as I left Guyana for the United States to pursue my graduate studies in public health, and while I completed my stint with the government of Guyana, I kept this special event in focus.

The measure of success achieved during my ministry served to further confirm my call to this noble vocation. Through His providential workings, God

Thy Will Be Done

had indeed confirmed my call. And on September 25, 2005, I was ordained to the Gospel ministry along with six other pastors.

I vividly remember preaching the divine hour message on the morning of my ordination and conducting the first baptism in a crusade that I was conducting in the village of Sophia on the outskirts of the city. After I was through with the baptism, I rushed home to prepare for the ordination service.

The ordination service was a most memorable occasion. Friends and colleagues who had witnessed my growth in ministry from my very early years, as well as a wide cross-section of the constituency, were in attendance. I was truly humbled by this show of support. The service took place at the Olivet Seventh-day Adventist Church. Elder Eugene Daniel, the Caribbean Union Conference president, and Pastor Andrew Farrell, family life director and ministerial secretary of the Caribbean Union Conference, along with representatives from the Guyana Conference administration, directorship, and the pastoral staff officiated during the service.

As I stood among the other pastors to be ordained, and later gave the Ordinands' Response, I felt a great sense of accomplishment. I was overwhelmed that God had chosen to confer on me this special approbation with all the privileges that ordination brings. It was an awe inspiring occasion. I glorified God for His great love and grace, towards me and thanked Him for being able to experience this highpoint in ministry.

In less than a year after my ordination, I was issued a license from the government granting me permission to perform wedding ceremonies.

After my ordination, I served as pastor at the Olivet SDA Church for two additional years. Then, immediately after the conference session of 2007, I was reassigned to the Ephesus SDA Church in the city.

In many respects, shepherding the flock at Ephesus was one of the high points of my pastoral ministry. During my ministry to that congregation, we saw the achievement of a number of milestones and experienced God's blessings in significant ways. It was one of the most fulfilling and enjoyable periods in my entire ministry. My pastoral responsibilities at Ephesus ended in July 2011.

Chapter 24

Stint with Caribbean Union College Extension Campus in Guyana

In late 2005 the Caribbean Union College administration approached me and asked that I coordinate the setting up of a CUC extension campus in Guyana to fill a need for Seventh-day Adventist tertiary education in my homeland. Because of economic constraints facing the Guyanese population, it was believed that the establishment of a campus in Guyana would result in a larger number of Guyanese benefiting from the college's program offerings.

In the beginning stages, the extension campus would offer two full degrees: a bachelor's degree in behavioral sciences and a bachelor's degree in elementary education. While the behavioral sciences degree was to be taught as a four-year degree, the elementary education degree was targeted to teachers in Guyana who had already completed two years of teachers' college training. By taking classes for two years at CUC, they would be able to earn a bachelor's degree.

Beyond these two complete program offerings, a student could begin any of the other degree programs offered on the main campus by completing the general education requirements in Guyana and then transferring to Trinidad to complete their degree studies.

I seized the opportunity and got to work immediately. With just about six weeks before the projected starting date of classes, I began by initiating contact with the relevant authorities in Guyana, including the Ministry of Education, the Cyril Potter College of Education, and the National Accreditation Council of Guyana (NACG). I simultaneously launched a promotional campaign designed to recruit students from among the churches countrywide and the community at large. This was followed by the recruitment of qualified lecturers to teach the respective courses.

Through God's providential workings, the college was able to rent space at the Josel Education Institute situated at the corner of 121 Peter Rose and Laluni Streets, Queenstown, Georgetown, from which the extension campus could be operated. Classes were initially scheduled between 4:30 p.m. to 9:00 p.m., Monday through Thursday.

God blessed our efforts, and in January 2006 the doors of the extension campus were opened with its first batch of eighteen students. The extension site was officially launched in February of that same year. Officials from CUC, the Guyana Conference of Seventh-day Adventists, the Ministry of Education, the Cyril Potter College of Education, the University of Guyana, private educational institutions, and other organizations attended the launching ceremony at the Josel's Education Institute. The Minister of Education gave the feature address during which he challenged CUC to assist in meeting the educational needs of the Guyanese people who would otherwise be unable to acquire a quality tertiary education.

Toward the end of that same month, Caribbean Union College achieved university status and was renamed the University of the Southern Caribbean (USC).

The enrollment at the extension campus has more than doubled since its doors were opened. A number of students who began studying at the extension campus have since transferred to the main campus in Trinidad to complete their degree studies. Several of them have already completed their study program there.

In 2010, the extension campus changed locations and moved into an independent building on Laluni Street. It has since increased its program offerings.

The first batch of students to have completed their degree studies in elementary education and behavioral science through the extension campus graduated during the USC main campus graduation ceremony in May, 2012.

During my term as Coordinator of the extension campus, the ground work for the registration of the campus was laid. In 2009, an application for registration with the NACG was submitted to that body. And in 2010, the extension campus was granted full registration status with the NACG.

I resigned my position as extension site coordinator in December 2009 after accepting a new position at Davis Memorial Hospital.

Chapter 25

Leadership Role at Davis Memorial Hospital

During the latter part of 2009, the chief executive officer of Davis Memorial Hospital (DMH) accepted a call to serve at the Caribbean Union Conference headquarters in Trinidad. In order to find a new CEO for the hospital, the board put together a search committee and tasked it with the responsibility of presenting to the board, a short list of candidates from which a new CEO would be selected at the board's November meeting that same year. The board appointed me as a member of the search committee.

The board chairman took the lead in the search process and conducted a number of interviews with a cross-section of the employees at DMH, church leaders, board members, and others. By the time the first search committee meeting was convened, the board chair had a list of eleven or twelve names that he was ready to share with the members of the search committee.

When the board chair read the names on the list, my name was mentioned among the set. I was dumbfounded. I sat quietly in my seat and tried to make sense of this new revelation. At that stage in my life, the prospects of serving as the CEO of DMH was nowhere in my thoughts. My mind began to race.

A few days before, while in attendance at an Executive Committee meeting of the Guyana Conference, Dr. Hilton Garnett, the conference president, officially announced that the DMH chief executive officer had recently been appointed to his new position at the Caribbean Union Conference headquarters and that the hospital board was searching for a new CEO. At the end of his announcement, I distinctly remembered him saying jestingly, "I hope that they do not call Pastor Isaacs." I simply dismissed such a notion.

After announcing the names, the board chairman, allowed for discussions on each name. I exited the meeting room when my name came up for discussion.

When I re-entered the room after the deliberations, the search committee short-listed three names, and my name was included on that list.

At that point in my career, I was preoccupied with my roles as conference

Thy Will Be Done

health ministries director and Adventist Development and Relief Agency (ADRA) Guyana country director. I was working on a number of initiatives that engaged my undivided attention. I, therefore, had not entertained any thought of changing jobs at that time. Rather, I was in the consolidation and expansion modes.

Even though I knew fully well that God would provide for His work, if I had to give up my positions, I was preoccupied with the thought of what would happen should I have to leave at that time. Then there was my involvement with the USC extension site and my pastoral role at the Ephesus Church in the city, not to mention, my involvement with various NGOs and other groups. The more I thought about the prospect of assuming the CEO position, the more concerned I became. I, therefore, made this a matter of much prayer and fasting.

During the period leading up to the DMH November board meeting, I carefully and prayerfully examined the pros and cons of accepting the offer to serve as the new CEO of the hospital. I also consulted with others on the matter.

I experienced a great degree of consternation in trying to come to grips with the probability of being offered the job at the hospital. I voiced my concerns to the Lord again and again as I tried to make sense of what was happening. I was not naive about the awesome responsibility and demands that were inherent in the position itself. He had led me to be placed in my current positions. Now He seemed to be indicating a new direction for my life.

After much reflection, prayer, and fasting, by the time of the hospital board's November meeting, I had gradually come around to the point where I was willing to accept the position after all, once it was offered to me. I concluded that if God chose to place me in that position, His will be done. I made a truce with Him that I would watch the selection process closely and should I be offered the position, I would accept it as His will for my life at that juncture.

The search committee completed its work and made a recommendation to the board at its mid-November meeting that I be appointed to the CEO position at the hospital to fill the existing vacancy. The board unanimously endorsed the recommendation, and voted my appointment. I was thus appointed as CEO of Davis Memorial Hospital with effect from January 1, 2010. I accepted the appointment willingly and began making plans for my transition.

With this new assignment, it occurred to me that there was no way I could continue shouldering all my existing responsibilities simultaneously with the CEO position. I first relinquished my position as the USC extension site coordinator. Next, I negotiated with the board to allow me to carry out maintenance

Leadership Role at Davis Memorial Hospital

activities as health ministries director and ADRA country director of the Guyana Conference for three months, or until such time that replacements were found.

Then, because of my deep sense of, and belief in, my call to the gospel ministry, I requested permission to be allowed to continue with my pastoral assignment at the Ephesus SDA Church simultaneously with my role as CEO of the hospital, and the request was granted.

On January 1, 2010, I assumed duties as CEO of Davis Memorial Hospital. This was not by any means a totally new area of responsibility for me. My stint as coordinator of health services at SIMAP Agency came in quite useful. Also, my graduate training in public health, especially the international health major, found ready application. In addition, I immersed myself in reading some good books on the subject of hospital administration, and I sought the advice and guidance of board members.

Of great help to me also in my early orientation to hospital administration, was my participation in a one-week workshop on hospital leadership organized by Adventist Health International and conducted in Honduras. This workshop was strategically conducted just two weeks into my new job. God, through His providential workings, had no doubt lined that up for me when I needed it most.

Following closely on the heels of the workshop in Honduras, I completed a one-semester graduate certificate course in Global Program Management and Evaluation from the University of Washington via online streaming from the university's International Training and Education Center for Health (I-TECH) Guyana office. This course was very useful to me since it offered me new insights into management. The learning acquired through that course found ready application on the job. I even benefitted from advice given by the executive director of I-TECH in my attempts to resolve problems on the job which threatened to disrupt the smooth flow of operations at the hospital.

When the situations warranted, I consulted with the former CEOs of the hospital. The board chair was a good mentor to me. Even though I felt a great deal of confidence in discharging my duties as CEO, I relied on the Lord for wisdom and understanding to be able to manage the affairs of the hospital well and deal with difficult situations.

During my two-year stint at DMH, I dedicated my time and energies to my job. I labored tirelessly for the constituency, the board, and the employees in my assigned tasks as CEO. Also, the patients and their families greatly benefited.

I completed the development of and implementation of a new business plan for the hospital; played a lead role in the recruitment of qualified staff;

re-established the human resources department; fostered the enhancement of the physical appearance of the hospital; and spearheaded the development of a hospital website. The hospital's finances also improved.

I also placed a lot of emphasis on missionary outreach activities and was integrally involved in the coordination of visits from overseas missionary groups. A number of missionary groups from overseas conducted outreach activities at DMH in collaboration with the Guyana Conference of SDA.

One of the most impacting of the missionary outreach initiatives took place in 2010, when the Legacy of Healing mission team from the United States visited Guyana. Arguably, it was the largest missionary outreach of its kind to ever hit Guyana's shores. Within a four-day period more than 152 free surgeries were performed at the hospital by a team of seven surgeons with support from five other medical practitioners who were all part of the group. A few surgeries were also conducted in the interior of the country where access to specialized medical care is very limited. Other team members, including nurses, anesthesiologists, and health educators simultaneously provided a wide variety of medical screening and evangelistic outreach activities at a number of strategic locations throughout the country.

Two major community collaborations that were effected during my time were the establishment of a memorandum of understanding between DMH and the US Peace Corps and the Guyana Safe Injection Project (GSIP) respectively. I was also instrumental in getting the Loma Linda University School of Medicine Class of 2011 to adopt DMH. Through the class' fund-raising efforts to benefit the hospital, a special fund was set up to provide financial assistance to needy patients who visit the hospital from time to time to access services but who cannot afford the hospital bills.

Each year, in an effort to keep the Guyanese in the diaspora abreast with developments taking place at DMH, I traveled to North America along with representatives from the Guyana Conference of Seventh-day Adventists, and presented reports to gatherings in New York, Massachusetts, Georgia, and Canada. At those gatherings donations were given to assist with the work at DMH. These overseases Guyanese groups also supported the hospital by funding various projects from time to time.

A building committee was established to accelerate the planning process for the construction of a new state-of-the-art building on the hospital compound. At the point of my leaving DMH, the committee was working feverishly toward the achievement of that objective.

While serving at DMH I learned by experience that being the CEO of a hospital is a complex and difficult task, and moving it forward is a rough road.

Leadership Role at Davis Memorial Hospital

Notwithstanding such challenges, with God's help, I was able to weather the storms.

Chapter 26

New Responsibilities in the Caribbean Union

The implementation of the hospital's strategic plan was moving apace. As a matter of fact, several aspects of the plan were being realized with rapidity. There was activity in almost every area of operations at the hospital. I was amazed at the rapidity at which the plans were moving ahead. I was settling into my new role quite nicely and was really enjoying my work, despite a few challenges here and there.

In June 2011, while in New York presenting a report to the overseas-based Guyanese on the work at DMH, one of my friends asked, "Pastor, with all these accomplishments taking place at the hospital what do you anticipate your next step will be in regards to moving on to something else after you are through with this phase of your life?" Since I did not have a ready answer to his question, I simply muttered something under my breath.

In July of that same year, I led a delegation from Davis Memorial Hospital to the Caribbean Union Conference's 15th Quinquennial Session which was held in Trinidad. When I left Guyana, I had every intention of returning to DMH to continue my work there. The session's meetings were moving along quite smoothly as officers and directors were being elected to the various positions.

On the penultimate day of the session, I was elected to serve as the new health ministries director of the Caribbean Union. I was taken by surprise. With this sudden change of circumstances, I had to start thinking about how I would transition out of my current role to assume my new responsibilities at the union. There were several key initiatives which we were engaged in at the hospital at that time that warranted my guidance and input in order for them to be fully realized. Foremost among them was the Positively United to Support Humanity (PUSH) project.

Earlier in the year, DMH had filed an application to the U.S. Centers for Disease Control and Prevention, through the United States President's Emergency Plan for AIDS Relief (PEPFAR), to be the prime grantee for a major grant to implement the PUSH project. PUSH, a five-year holistic HIV care and treatment initiative, was the bringing together of a consortium of faith-based partners in Guyana led by DMH, to continue strengthening and expanding HIV care, treatment, and support services begun under AIDS Relief. At that time, AIDS Relief was about to end its operations in Guyana.

Once this project was funded there would need to be a heavy investment of time and energies to get it up and running. In anticipation of the announcement of the award, systems were being put in place to ensure that the project got underway on the proposed start date of September 1. Apart from this, once the project got underway, it would require close monitoring and supervision, especially in its early stages, to ensure that it was being implemented according to schedule. The hospital was gearing up to spring into action once the funding was received.

Apart from PUSH, another initiative at the hospital that was occupying my attention when I was elected to my new position at the Caribbean Union, was negotiating a call for a Filipino couple (both physicians) to join DMH as missionary doctors. To allow for a smooth transition to Guyana once the call was accepted, I needed to ensure that the requisite mechanisms were in place for their relocation to Guyana. From a practical standpoint, therefore, I could not arbitrarily give up my current responsibilities at the hospital immediately to take up my new appointment at the Union. The hospital board held a similar view.

Through negotiations between the new administration of the Caribbean Union and the Davis Memorial Hospital board, a consensus was reached whereby I was allowed to remain in my substantive position as CEO of the hospital until December 31, 2011. This was with the understanding that I would assume full-time duties at the Caribbean Union on January 1, 2012.

Approximately two weeks after my election to my new position at the Union, DMH was awarded the grant from the CDC. The project started on schedule. It was officially launched on November 8 with an impressive ceremony at which the minister of health gave the feature address.

I devoted a significant portion of my time to the PUSH project to ensure that it was implemented as smoothly as possible. This was a noteworthy achievement for the hospital, its partners, and Guyana as a whole. As far as I am aware, this was the first time that the U.S. Centers for Disease Control and Prevention had directly funded an initiative of such a magnitude that was led by a local faith-based group in Guyana. PUSH therefore placed DMH on the map as a grant recipient and marked a new era in the life of the hospital.

The two doctors from the Philippines, en-route from Ghana, where they were serving, accepted the call to serve at DMH and joined our staff in

Thy Will Be Done

mid-November. As it turned out, the couple's daughter, a registered nurse, accompanied them from Ghana along with her infant son, and joined the hospital's staff as a full-time nurse.

In an effort to foster the work of the health ministries department of the union, I conducted a select number of health ministry activities and programs in a few fields simultaneously with my work at DMH. I also attended relevant meetings and represented the union at workshops and seminars both in the Caribbean and overseas.

On January 1, 2012, I assumed full-time responsibilities as health ministries director of the Caribbean Union and have since been working feverishly to push ahead with various initiatives.

In March 2012, the Caribbean Union Executive Committee appointed me to the position of ADRA Director concurrently with my responsibility for health ministries.

Interestingly, while in the process of packing our household and personal effects in preparation for shipment to Trinidad, I came across a letter that I had written to the president of the Caribbean Union in 1998 asking to fill the positions of health ministries and ADRA director of the union at the end of my graduate studies at Loma Linda University on account of the expertise being acquired. Actually, the letter was merely a class assignment for one of my courses that had to do with writing job applications and résumé and was, therefore, never mailed. I marvel at how this notion became a reality fourteen years later. Further, I am more conscious now than ever before that indeed words and thoughts have molding powers and that one should be careful about what one asks for in life.

My new assignments at the union and our family's relocation to Trinidad will no doubt open up new vistas . Our three children who are of college, secondary, and primary school ages respectively, will be able to enjoy the special privilege of receiving a Christian education.

I view my new responsibilities at the Caribbean Union as the opening up of a new chapter in God's plan for my life.

Chapter 27

God Is Not Finished With Me Yet

As I look back over the course of my life up to this point, I am amazed at what God has helped me to accomplish despite my humble beginnings and the setbacks I suffered along the way. Amidst the vicissitudes of my life, I have seen the guiding hand of God at work as I sought to discover and do His will. What I have become in this life is due in no small way to God. Over the years, He has been molding and fashioning me. I have had a very successful ministry. I have sought to live my life as an example of how God's will can be achieved in one's life.

Moreover my life has been an exciting journey with God. The struggles experienced in sorting out and following His will for my life at different points along the way, the joy of discovering and doing His will, my academic and professional accomplishments, and my work experience with the civic society and the SDA Church, have all contributed toward the special tapestry that God has woven into my life. As I look back in retrospect, I am humbled at what God has wrought on my behalf.

Further, having the assurance that I am serving in a place where God would have me be gives me a sense of joy, satisfaction, and peace of mind. My desire is to be where God would have me be and serve where He would have me serve.

I do not claim to have achieved all that God has mapped out for my life, for I am quite aware that "the path of the just is as the shining light, that shineth more and more unto the perfect day" (Prov. 4:18).

As I continue to serve in His vineyard, my motto is "To do His will." My prayer is, "Father, lead me day by day, ever in Thine own sweet way, teach me to be pure and true, show me what I ought to do."

Based on my experience with the Lord over the years, when faced with uncertainties, I have the conviction that He will help me to make the best decisions in the prevailing circumstances. Therefore, in such situations, I do not worry too much, neither am afraid of the outcome. I simply leave everything in God's hands and follow His lead.

Thy Will Be Done

I have learned oftentimes, God does not reveal the entire plan for one's life all at once, instead, He does so gradually along life's journey. I have also learned that keeping in tune with God is crucial in being able to discern His will and purposes for my life at every stage. What God has in store for me for the remainder of my life is yet to be seen. But one thing I know for sure. He is not finished with me yet!

We invite you to view the complete
selection of titles we publish at:

www.TEACHServices.com

Scan with your mobile
device to go directly
to our website.

Please write or email us your praises, reactions,
or thoughts about this or any other book we publish at:

www.TEACHServices.com • (800) 367-1844

P.O. Box 954
Ringgold, GA 30736

info@TEACHServices.com

TEACH Services, Inc., titles may be purchased in bulk for
educational, business, fund-raising, or sales promotional use.
For information, please e-mail:

BulkSales@TEACHServices.com

Finally, if you are interested in seeing
your own book in print, please contact us at

publishing@TEACHServices.com

We would be happy to review your manuscript for free.

www.ingramcontent.com/pod-product-compliance
Lightning Source LLC
Chambersburg PA
CBHW070540170426
43200CB00011B/2492